The Giant Book of Random Facts

By
Jake Jacobs

Kindle Edition

* * * * *

Published by Jake Jacobs at Amazon Kindle

1.

Eminem's alter ego, Slim Shady, was created so his band could have 12 members.

Reference: (https://en.wikipedia.org/wiki/D12)

2.

The movie "Project X" has spawned several grandiose parties in attempts to recreate it, resulting in some parties causing millions of dollars in damages, one death, and dozens of drug overdoses.

Reference: (https://en.wikipedia.org/wiki/Project_X_(2012_film)#Impact)

3.

Specific rifles were made to sell to Native Americas that were smooth bored, making them less accurate.

Reference: (https://en.wikipedia.org/wiki/Model_1814_common_rifle)

4.

In 2010, a paper was published that proved mathematically that giraffes are able to swim, but only barely.

Reference: (http://scienceblogs.com/tetrapodzoology/2010/06/02/giraffe-flotation-dynamics/)

5.

AutoBrewery Syndrome causes carbohydrates to ferment into ethanol, making one involuntarily drunk.

Reference: (http://edition.cnn.com/2013/09/19/health/gut-fermentation-syndrome/)

6.

The Queens actual title is "Elizabeth the Second, by the Grace of God, of the United Kingdom of Great Britain and Northern Ireland and of Her other Realms and Territories Queen, Head of the Commonwealth, Defender of the Faith."

Reference: (http://news.bbc.co.uk/2/hi/programmes/monarchy/2013159.stm)

7.

A penguin escaped from Tokyo Sea Life Park and thrived in Tokyo Bay for 82 days after scaling the 13 foot high wall and managing to get through a barbed-wire fence into the bay. The penguin, known only by its number, 337, was later recaptured by the zoo keepers.

Reference: (https://en.wikipedia.org/wiki/Humboldt_penguin#Escape_from_Tokyo_Zoo)

8.

Porky Pig's original voice actor, Joe Dougherty, had a natural stutter. This made recording sessions long and production costs higher due to the fact that he could not control his stutter. He was eventually replaced in 1937 by Mel Blanc, the voice of Bugs Bunny.

Reference: (https://en.wikipedia.org/wiki/Porky_Pig)

9.

"The Ford Show" was a television variety program hosted by Tennessee Ernie Ford, and was sponsored by the Ford Motor Company.

Reference: (https://en.wikipedia.org/wiki/The_Ford_Show)

10.

In 2015, two primatologists working in the forests of the Republic of Congo, took the first-ever photograph of the Bouvier's red colobus monkey, a rare primate not seen for more than half a century and suspected to be extinct.

Reference: (http://press.wcs.org/News-Releases/articleType/ArticleView/articleId/6689/April-16-Critically-Endangered-Monkey-Photographed-In-Congos-Newest-National-Park-Ntokou-Pikounda.aspx)

11.

Chicken eggs from the United States would be illegal in Europe and vice versa. Legislation in the United States requires eggs to be washed for hygienic reasons and stored in refrigerator whereby the European Union forbids washing because it removes the natural protective cuticle.

Reference: (https://www.popsugar.com/food/Should-You-Refrigerate-Eggs-43834826)

12.

When Brad Bird approached Lily Tomlins to voice Edna Mode in "The Incredibles," she first listened to Bird's voiceover work for the character and responded by asking him what he needed her for when he already captured the character perfectly.

Reference: (https://en.wikipedia.org/wiki/List_of_The_Incredibles_characters#Edna_Mode)

13.

Webers, a restaurant on an Ontario highway, was so popular that travelers risked death running across the highway and climbing over the median for its burgers. The owner bought a Toronto footbridge and moved it over the highway to prevent injury.

Reference: (https://en.wikipedia.org/wiki/Webers)

14.

Under the law of the United Kingdom; whales, dolphins, porpoises and sturgeons are royal fish, and when taken, become the personal property of the monarch. Under current law, the Receiver of Wreck is the official appointed to take possession of royal fish when they arrive on English shores.

Reference: (https://en.wikipedia.org/wiki/Royal_fish?oldformat=true)

15.

There is a species of crayfish that mutated 25 years ago in an aquarium and has the ability to reproduce by cloning itself. It is now an invasive species working its way across Europe and Asia.

Reference: (https://www.nature.com/articles/s41559-018-0467-9)

16.

12 months following D. B. Cooper's successful hijacking, there were 15 unsuccessful copycat attempts.

Reference: (https://en.wikipedia.org/wiki/D._B._Cooper)

17.

Australian researchers discovered that drinking a cup of pear juice before drinking alcohol resulted in fewer and diminished hangover symptoms the next day.

Reference: (http://www.esquire.com/food-drink/drinks/a36965/pear-juice-hangover-cure/)

18.

Canadians have an annual death race, a 125 kilometer race through the Rockies, but no one has ever died.

Reference: (http://www.canadiandeathrace.com/what-is-the-canadian-death-race)

19.

There is a medical condition that can cause sufferers to taste the words they hear. The condition is called synesthesia.

Reference: (https://en.wikipedia.org/wiki/Synesthesia)

20.

NPR CarTalk Tom Magliozzi's grave stone has, "It's not hard work that killed him", inscribed in Latin.

Reference: (https://www.findagrave.com/memorial/138246898/thomas-louis-magliozzi)

21.

The United States believed in 1950 that Communist conventional forces massively outnumbered the West. Despite nuclear weapons American planners feared that even Britain would have to be abandoned during a Soviet invasion, a possibility that they didn't discuss with their British counterparts.

Reference: (https://en.wikipedia.org/wiki/Single_Integrated_Operational_Plan#Truman)

22.

Richard Ayoade, who plays Moss in "The IT Crowd," wrote two plays with John Oliver in the late 1990s when they were in the same theatre group.

Reference: (https://en.wikipedia.org/wiki/Richard_Ayoade#Early_career)

23.

Hachiko the dog loyally waited for his deceased owner to return for 9 years.

Reference: (https://en.wikipedia.org/wiki/Hachik%C5%8D)

24.

Alicia Vikander is married to Michael Fassbender.

Reference: (https://en.wikipedia.org/wiki/Alicia_Vikander)

25.

Samsung, the famous cell phone and television manufacturer, started off as a grocery store.

Reference: (http://www.complex.com/pop-culture/2013/05/50-things-you-didnt-know-about-samsung/originally-a-grocery-store-business)

26.

The mail clerks on the Titanic are likely to have died trying to save the mail from the rising water.

Reference:(https://en.wikipedia.org/wiki/Sinking_of_the_RMS_Titanic#Departure_of_the_lifeboats_.2800:45.E2.80.9302:05.29)

27.

Teddy Roosevelt was once shot in the chest and after his attacker was disarmed, he calmly asked him why he did it. Roosevelt then went on to give a scheduled 90 minute speech before seeking medical attention.

Reference: (http://www.history.com/news/shot-in-the-chest-100-years-ago-teddy-roosevelt-kept-on-talking)

28.

You'd have to click a mouse roughly 10 million times to burn 1 calorie.

Reference: (https://www.wired.com/story/you-dont-burn-one-calorie-clicking-a-mouse)

29.

The Silent Hill video game was based on the town of Centralia, Pennsylvania.

Reference: (http://www.blumhouse.com/2015/11/18/silent-hill-town-based-on-the-real-life-story-of-centralia-pa/)

30.

Japan's educations minister asked 50 Japanese universities to chop down their humanities and social science departments. 26 universities said that they will comply.

Reference: (http://www.theguardian.com/higher-education-network/2015/sep/25/japans-humanities-chop-sends-shivers-down-academic-spines)

31.

The United States government has a secret airline that flies to many classified bases in Nevada.

Reference: (https://www.youtube.com/watch?v=pWNGAUvSyOc)

32.

Blackbeard, the pirate, and his crew would lock themselves in the hold of the ship and light pots of Sulphur to see who could last the longest without suffocating.

Reference: (http://markstrecker.com/page8.html)

33.

With an attendance of 44,710, the 2014 Canadian Football Grey Cup championship game in Regina would have qualified as the third-largest city in Saskatchewan.

Reference: (http://news.nationalpost.com/sports/cfl/grey-cup-2013-saskatchewan-roughriders-coronation-at-hamilton-tiger-cats-expense-feels-like-spring-in-more-ways-than-one)

34.

Steven Seagal broke Sean Connery's wrist during the training for James Bond's "Never Say Never Again."

Reference: (https://en.wikipedia.org/wiki/Never_Say_Never_Again)

35.

Carl's Jr. is called Hardee's on the east coast and vice versa on the west coast.

Reference: (http://mentalfloss.com/article/63291/whats-difference-between-hardees-and-carls-jr)

36.

The average birthday of all U.S. Presidents so far is July 4th.

Reference: (https://gist.github.com/anonymous/c1c5cc9302214dd0402032eec6ea5b2b)

37.

Until 1992, it wasn't required for electrical appliances in Britain to be sold with plugs at the end. Often, the consumer had to attach it themselves.

Reference: (http://articles.philly.com/1992-01-31/news/26033529_1_plug-royal-society-domestic-electrical-appliances)

38.

Superman once went to Eternia and fought He-Man while being controlled by a Skeletor spell.

Reference: (http://he-man.wikia.com/wiki/From_Eternia_--_With_Death!)

39.

The city Eridu was finally abandoned in the 6th century B.C., but existed on and off for almost 5,000 years before that.

Reference: (https://en.wikipedia.org/wiki/Eridu)

40.

The Olympic Games have an official anthem.

Reference: (https://www.youtube.com/watch?v=fVT-WNbSZig)

41.

French preschools serve four-course lunches, including a cheese course, to educate them in taste and stimulate their senses.

Reference: (http://www.houstonchronicle.com/local/gray-matters/article/How-French-kids-acquire-a-taste-for-life-And-6738096.php?t=ae7d9c3ae2438d9cbb)

42.

Devo used to open for their own concert as the Christian band "Dove, The Band of Love." They would play Christian versions of their songs.

Reference:(http://dangerousminds.net/comments/dove_the_band_of_love_devos_christian_alter_ego)

43.

Oscar Niemeyer, the Brazilian architect responsible for designing its capital of Brasilia, lived to almost 105. Starting in the 1930s, Niemeyer's career spanned nine decades. Yuri Gagarin, the Russian cosmonaut and first man in space, said his city, "was like arriving on another planet".

Reference: (https://www.reuters.com/article/us-brazil-niemeyer/brazilian-architect-oscar-niemeyer-dies-aged-104-idUSBRE8B501920121206)

44.

There's an island in Japan where you can cook in a volcano.

Reference: (https://www.youtube.com/watch?v=-N5pqG7-qDY)

45.

In 2005, security guards at Australia's Parliament House were banned from calling people "mate". The ban lasted one day.

Reference: (http://www.theage.com.au/news/national/they-tried-to-ban-mate-but-no-one-has-the-guts/2005/08/19/1124435143831.html)

46.

Prince's name change wasn't just a PR stunt, it was part of an attempt to be free from Warner Music's control.

Reference: (http://www.theguardian.com/music/2015/aug/10/history-prince-contractual-controversy-warner-paisley-park)

47.

About half the population sits while they wipe when going to the bathroom and the other half stands. Interestingly, most people don't know the other group exists.

Reference: (https://deadspin.com/5424415/sitters-vs-standers--the-great-wipe-hope)

48.

Mount Kosciuszko was thought to be the highest mountain in Australia until Mount Townsend was found to be slightly taller. Rather than re-educating the public that Townsend was the new highest mountain, the New South Wales Lands Department simply switched their names.

Reference: (https://en.wikipedia.org/wiki/Mount_Townsend)

49.

A horse's hoof is basically a big fingernail, and they run along on the tip of a single toe.

Reference: (http://scienceline.ucsb.edu/getkey.php?key=5456)

50.

John Wilkes Booth's father's middle name was Brutus, named after the infamous assassin of Julius Caesar.

Reference: (https://en.wikipedia.org/wiki/Marcus_Junius_Brutus_the_Younger#Legacy)

51.

Michael Jackson has two sons, Prince Michael Jackson I and Prince Michael Jackson II.

Reference: (http://www.huffingtonpost.com/2013/03/12/michael-jacksons-kids-prince-paris-blanket_n_2862437.html?m=false)

52.

We can get a ship to Mars in 9 months or less, depending on current orbit positions for both Earth and Mars.

Reference: (https://www.space.com/24701-how-long-does-it-take-to-get-to-mars.html)

53.

During World War I, the British Army began calling their Mark 1 battle tanks "tanks," in order to mislead German intelligence into believing the vehicles held water.

Reference: (https://www.iwm.org.uk/history/how-britain-invented-the-tank-in-the-first-world-war)

54.

The American robin is a key host of the West Nile virus and is largely responsible among birds for transmitting the disease to humans.

Reference: (https://www.sciencedaily.com/releases/2009/02/090220191318.htm)

55.

Eminem rapped about antacid in three different songs, making him the artist to mention the word the most in his raps.

Reference: (http://www.lyrics.net/lyrics/antacids)

56.

RMS Queen Mary ran over the HMS Curacoa after the Curacoa made a navigation error while helping it evade submarine attacks.

Reference: (https://en.wikipedia.org/wiki/HMS_Curacoa_(D41)#Collision)

57.

François Clemmons, "Officer Clemmons" from Mister Rogers' Neighborhood, was gay, but Mister Rogers did not permit him to be "out" on the show and suggested he get married as a cover.

Reference: (https://en.wikipedia.org/wiki/Fran%C3%A7ois_Clemmons#Personal_life)

58.

The digestive biscuit, or cookies in the United States, were first made as a dietary aid, and that's where they got their name.

Reference: (https://en.wikipedia.org/wiki/Digestive_biscuit#History)

59.

Prince gave a free, surprise show for handicapped students at Gallaudet College. The concert was his idea, and apparently he asked for no media coverage.

Reference: (https://www.washingtonpost.com/archive/local/1984/11/30/prince-regales-handicapped-students/59494e6e-df41-4313-b252-99306cd91376/)

60.

Some Muslims don't celebrate birthdays. They consider the act an "innovation" or addition to their practices and thus consider it a sin. These are typically Salafists.

Reference: (https://en.wikipedia.org/wiki/Birthday#Islam)

61.

Annually, human sources emit over 100 times more carbon dioxide than volcanic eruptions do.

Reference: (https://www.scientificamerican.com/article/earthtalks-volcanoes-or-humans/)

62.

Tobacco smokers have a much lower rate of suffering from Parkinson's disease and nobody knows why.

Reference: (https://en.wikipedia.org/wiki/Parkinson%27s_disease)

63.

Delaware has 50,000 more corporations than people.

Reference: (http://www.nytimes.com/2012/07/01/business/how-delaware-thrives-as-a-corporate-tax-haven.html?referer=https:/www.bing.com/search?q=1209%20north%20orange%20street%20delaware%20new%20York%20times&pivot=web&persona=0&input=1&form=SBCLIK2&mkt=en-US&setlang=en-US)

64.

According to the CDC, lumberjacks are among the top people most likely to commit suicide.

Reference: (https://www.cbsnews.com/news/these-jobs-have-the-highest-rate-of-suicide/)

65.

President Lyndon B. Johnson was a competitive womanizer, and whenever people mentioned Kennedy's many affairs, Johnson would bang the table and declare that he had more women by accident than Kennedy ever had on purpose.

Reference: (https://www.theatlantic.com/magazine/archive/1998/04/three-new-revelations-about-lbj/377094/)

66.

Studio Ghibli was originally going to produce a movie based on Little Nemo: Adventures in Slumberland, but left the project based on differences Miyazaki had with the producers.

Reference: (http://www.slashfilm.com/watch-scene-studio-ghiblis-abandoned-little-nemo-dreamland/)

67.

Best Friends Animals Society has reduced the number of animals killed in Utah shelters from 46,000 a year to less than 4,000 by advocating spaying and neutering programs and promoting adoption programs. They also have over 3,700 acres of land dedicated to homeless animals.

Reference: (http://bestfriends.org/about/faqs#Sanctuary4)

68.

In 2014, coffee prices doubled due to dry hot weather in Brazil, which produces 40% of the world's coffee beans. 30% of the crop may have been lost in the worst drought in 50 years.

Reference: (http://www.businessinsider.com/why-coffee-prices-are-surging-2014-2)

69.

Nietzsche criticized anti-Semitism and German nationalism, believing in his final years that he was, "a pure-blooded Polish nobleman, without a single drop of bad blood, certainly not German". He claimed he and Germany were great thanks to, "Polish blood in their veins", and wanted "all anti-Semites shot".

Reference: (https://en.wikipedia.org/wiki/%C3%9Cbermensch#Nazism)

70.

Nanotechnology could be used to keep fossil fuels clean and cut CO2 emissions.

Reference: (http://www.energyglobal.com/upstream/drilling-and-production/10072013/Nanotechnology_could_keep_coal_clean_261/#.Ud1zLutpURI)

71.

There are 7,097 living languages in the world and 918 of them are considered dying. The Americas are responsible for over one third of dying languages.

Reference: (http://www.ethnologue.com/world)

72.

Despite being used since the mid-19th century, scientists still don't know how anesthesia works.

Reference: (https://www.scientificamerican.com/article/how-does-anesthesia-work/)

73.

The Soviets repurposed the Beatles' hit "Can't Buy Me Love" to point to the hypocrisy of Western Capitalism, arguing that money and consumerism could indeed purchase love in the "West".

Reference: (http://www.bbc.co.uk/programmes/p02rh1km)

74.

Narwhal skin is an important source of vitamin C for the Inuit people. Ounce for ounce, there is almost as much vitamin C in narwhal skin as there is in an orange.

Reference: (http://www.bbc.co.uk/nature/humanplanetexplorer/environments/arctic)

75.

The Unclaimed Baggage Center in Scottsboro, Alabama, is where most of the United States' unclaimed baggage goes to.

Reference: (https://www.unclaimedbaggage.com/about/)

76.

There's a museum in Tokyo devoted to their sewer system, which is relatively recent, and one of the features is a deep basement level which has a bridge into a large, raw sewage pipe.

Reference: (http://onlyinjapan.tv/tokyo-museum-of-sewage/)

77.

Grover Cleveland was both the 22nd and 24th President of the United States and, when in office, married a 21 year old woman who was 28 years younger than himself.

Reference: (https://en.wikipedia.org/wiki/Presidencies_of_Grover_Cleveland)

78.

PT Barnum's, of Ringling and Barnum and Bailey's Circus, entrainment career began by showcasing an enslaved "161 year old woman."

Reference: (http://lostmuseum.cuny.edu/archive/exhibit/heth/)

79.

Even 16 years after the columbine shooting, the "basement tapes" of Eric Harris and Dylan Klebold were considered dangerous to the public and destroyed in early 2015.

Reference: (http://www.westword.com/news/columbine-killers-basement-tapes-destroyed-6283043)

80.

Many older people in Russia remember seeing and hearing strange vinyl type discs when they were young. The discs had partial images of skeletons on them, were called "Bones" or "Ribs" and originated in the Cold War years of the Soviet Union.

Reference: (https://www.x-rayaudio.com/x-rayaudioproject/)

81.

In the first official FIFA international game, England had 7 strikers while Scotland had 6. The game ended 0-0.

Reference: (http://www.fifa.com/live-scores/news/y=2012/m=11/news=the-birth-international-football-1959304.html)

82.

Michael Jackson nearly cancelled a concert in Moscow in 1993, after saboteurs reported hoax drugs and bomb scares to sabotage the event with police raids. Despite this, the torrential rain and the fact that the concert actually lost money, Michael Jackson did it anyway.

Reference: (http://www.truemichaeljackson.com/true-stories/concert-in-moscow/)

83.

Macau has a population density per square kilometer of 18,600, whereas Mongolia has 2.

Reference: (https://en.wikipedia.org/wiki/East_Asia)

84.

Cephalopods do not have a blind spot in their eyes due to evolving eyesight separately from vertebrates.

Reference: (https://en.wikipedia.org/wiki/Cephalopod_eye)

85.

Like smallpox, Polio is on its way out with 22 cases worldwide in 2017.

Reference: (https://en.wikipedia.org/wiki/Poliomyelitis_eradication)

86.

Henry Ford was given the award of the Grand Cross of the German Eagle, which is the highest medal Nazi Germany could bestow on a foreigner.

Reference: (https://en.wikipedia.org/wiki/Henry_Ford)

87.

There was an operation named Operation Mincemeat, which was a plan devised during World War II to give a corpse to Axis to feed them misinformation. This saved thousands of Ally lives and allowed an easier takedown of Mussolini.

Reference: (http://www.bbc.co.uk/history/topics/operation_mincemeat)

88.

Before being classified as a poison, ether was seen as an acceptable alternative to alcohol. In fact, 17,000 gallons were consumed in Ireland as a beverage. Ether also created serious social problems in Poland leading to school pupils being sent home due to intoxication.

Reference: (https://en.wikipedia.org/wiki/Ether_addiction#History)

89.

In Great Britain, 93,000 liters of beer are rumored to be lost each year in facial hair.

Reference: (http://discovermagazine.com/2013/june/21-20-things-you-didnt-know-about-beer)

90.

The emergency oxygen systems onboard passenger aircraft used chemical reaction to produce oxygen.

Reference: (https://en.wikipedia.org/wiki/Emergency_oxygen_system)

91.

In 1983, the Department of Justice stole people-tracking software from Inslaw Inc., programmed a back-door into the software, and sold it to foreign governments.

Reference: (http://www.wired.com/1993/01/inslaw/)

92.

Nearly 400 laboratories in the United States test products on 70,000 dogs per year. 96% are beagles due to their easy-going and non-resistant nature.

Reference: (http://bfp.org/about-bfp/)

93.

While researching his political comedy "In the Loop", writer Armando Iannucci, creator of Veep, sneaked into the U.S. State Department in Washington using a pass which he claims could have been produced by a child.

Reference: (http://www.telegraph.co.uk/news/worldnews/northamerica/usa/5295148/Comedian-sneaks-into-US-State-department.html)

94.

Kevin Spacey recorded his lines for the movie "Moon" in half a day.

Reference: (http://joeblade.com/2009/07/21/trivia-on-the-film-moon/)

95.

The father of the Soviet space race, Sergei Korolev, died 2 years before scheduling a man on the Moon, which would have been a year before the United States. Enthusiasm and funding from the Soviet leadership dried up following his death. He died from pushing himself too hard to compete with the United States.

Reference: (https://en.wikipedia.org/wiki/Sergei_Korolev#Human_spaceflight)

96.

The world's most expensive potato chips cost $11 each and come in a box of five.

Reference: (http://uk.businessinsider.com/st-eriks-brewery-worlds-most-expensive-potato-chip-taste-test-2016-11)

97.

The only member of the band ZZ Top who doesn't sport the iconic long beard the band is known for is also the only member whose last name is Beard.

Reference: (https://en.wikipedia.org/wiki/ZZ_Top)

98.

The United States detonated three nuclear weapons in outer space.

Reference: (https://en.wikipedia.org/wiki/Operation_Argus)

99.

Six states still give the option to be executed with the electric chair over lethal injection; the only 6 places in the entire world that still allow this. Virginia was the most recent to execute by electric chair in 2013.

Reference: (https://en.wikipedia.org/wiki/Electric_chair#Decline)

100.

McKinney North High School removed their bathroom doors in order to keep their students from having sex.

Reference: (https://www.huffingtonpost.com/2012/01/14/mckinney-school-district-denies-removing-bathroom-doors-to-prevent-students-from-having-sex-in-them_n_1206239.html?ncid=engmodushpmg00000006)

101.

Torch Lake, often compared to the Caribbean, is located in Michigan and is one of the clearest lakes in the world.

Reference: (http://www.mlive.com/travel/index.ssf/2017/07/torch_lake_facts.html)

102.

In Finland, they have "National Sleepy Head Day", where the last person in a family to wake up is thrown in to a lake or the sea by the rest of the family.

Reference: (https://en.wikipedia.org/wiki/National_Sleepy_Head_Day)

103.

The "Any Other Weapon" category of the U.S. National Firearms Act is a "catch-all" category for improvised firearms, disguised firearms, and pistols with a second vertical grip. They only require a $5 tax stamp from the BATFE rather than the $200 stamp for short barreled rifles and machine guns.

Reference: (https://en.wikipedia.org/wiki/Title_II_weapons#Any_other_weapon)

104.

Counterfeiters once plotted to steal President Lincoln's body to pressure the governor to release their best engraver from prison.

Reference: (https://www.usnews.com/news/articles/2007/06/24/a-plot-to-steal-lincolns-body)

105.

President Teddy Roosevelt was given strong coffee and puffs of cigar as a child to "help" with his asthma. As an adult his coffee drinking became legendary and he drank up to 40 cups per day. His son, Theodore Jr., remarked that his father's ideal coffee cup might be, "more in the nature of a bathtub".

Reference: (http://www.myrecipes.com/extracrispy/teddy-roosevelt-drank-an-unholy-amount-of-coffee)

106.

Nakagin Capsule Tower in Tokyo is one of the last remaining and rare examples of Japanese Metabolism, an architectural movement emblematic of Japan's postwar cultural resurgence.

Reference: (https://en.wikipedia.org/wiki/Nakagin_Capsule_Tower)

107.

Some people believe that they can read your fortune by examining your fecal matter.

Reference: (https://en.wikipedia.org/wiki/Scatomancy)

108.

In 1925, a man sued his wife Alice, who was black, on the basis that she had misled him into believing that she was a white woman. She was forced to undress in the courtroom to prove that her ancestry was obvious in an intimate setting, and won $32,000 in the divorce settlement.

Reference: (https://en.wikipedia.org/wiki/Kip_Rhinelander)

109.

Guns N' Roses' song "November Rain" was loosely based off a short story written by Del James, titled "Without You". It tells the story of a musician trying to cope with losing his loved one.

Reference: (http://www.mtv.com/news/2575935/six-things-you-didnt-know-about-guns-n-roses-november-rain/)

110.

Adding cold cream to your coffee actually keeps it warmer longer when compared to black coffee.

Reference: (http://www.thekitchn.com/surprising-science-why-adding-cold-cream-to-coffee-keeps-it-hotter-longer-195895)

111.

Italy and Poland bear mutual historical references and mention each other in their anthems in the adjective form.

Reference: (https://en.wikipedia.org/wiki/Italy%E2%80%93Poland_relations#20th_century)

112.

Unlike the United States and the United Kingdom, Germany abolished all academic gowns following the year 1967, when students protested under the slogan, "beneath the gowns the fug of 1000 years", against the academic habits they viewed as remnants of Nazism.

Reference: (https://en.wikipedia.org/wiki/Academic_dress#Germany)

113.

Inside neutron stars, nuclear material can form "nuclear pasta", where it exists in phases like the spaghetti and lasagna phase, so named for their resemblance to pasta.

Reference: (https://www.youtube.com/watch?v=euwtanuYoHA)

114.

Members of the Nation of Islam are encouraged to study Dianetics, which is the same philosophy that is central to Scientology and invented by L. Ron Hubbard.

Reference: (https://en.wikipedia.org/wiki/Nation_of_Islam)

115.

President Eisenhower wanted the United States Government to maintain a list of homosexual government employees as a countermeasure to attempted Soviet espionage.

Reference:(https://en.wikipedia.org/wiki/Martin_and_Mitchell_defection#Government_response)

116.

A Catholic priest was strangled and stomped to death while serving a prison sentence for sexually molesting over 130 children in the Boston area.

Reference: (https://en.wikipedia.org/wiki/John_Geoghan)

117.

Maniraptorans were feathered and sometimes beaked dinosaurs who were able to survive post-impact nuclear winter and evolve into birds by being omnivorous.

Reference: (https://en.wikipedia.org/wiki/Maniraptora)

118.

Reverend Kieran McHugh once stunned the 900 students of the private Pope John XXIII Regional High School when he told them that, effective immediately, they would have to dismantle their personal pages on sites such as MySpace.com and Xanga.com and any other blogs, or face suspension.

Reference: (http://www.mtv.com/news/1512215/catholic-school-principal-to-students-thou-shalt-not-blog/)

119.

Semi-trucks or tractor trailers average somewhere between 4 to 8 miles per gallon of fuel. Going up a hill it can dip to 2.9 miles per gallon, but going down a hill it can rise to 23 miles per gallon.

Reference: (https://www.popularmechanics.com/cars/trucks/gmp116/10-things-you-didnt-know-about-semi-trucks/)

120.

There's a medical condition called "Witzelsucht," where damage of the frontal lobe causes a tendency to make puns, or tell inappropriate jokes or pointless stories in socially inappropriate situations.

Reference: (https://en.wikipedia.org/wiki/Witzelsucht)

121.

The blonde girl, who distracts Manny in the movie "Scarface", vanished shortly after filming and has never been seen or heard from since.

Reference: (http://www.charleyproject.org/cases/l/leppert_tammy.html)

122.

African elephants can be easily distinguished from Asian elephants in that their ears have the shape of Africa.

Reference: (https://www.britannica.com/story/whats-the-difference-between-asian-and-african-elephants)

123.

During the Sack of Rome in 390 BC, the Romans were routed and the city was all but destroyed, however, the Romans figured that they could just pay the invaders to leave. It worked.

Reference: (https://en.wikipedia.org/wiki/Battle_of_the_Allia)

124.

The Monarch of Oman, Sultan Qaboos, has been questioned by Omanis to be homosexual. His homosexuality has been confirmed by Oman's second most senior intelligence officer.

Reference: (https://en.wikipedia.org/wiki/Qaboos_bin_Said_al_Said#Other_public_activities)

125.

It's legal to fire a missile in South Carolina with a permit, and the penalty for doing so without a permit is a $100 fine.

Reference: (http://www.scstatehouse.gov/code/t23c033.php)

126.

A California school district banned dictionaries after a student who was searching for the word "orangutan" came across the definition for "oral sex." They pulled dictionaries from the school for having "age inappropriate" words.

Reference: (http://www.foxnews.com/us/2010/01/27/california-school-district-bans-dictionary-oral-sex-definition.html)

127.

Originally, U.S. PC keyboards did not have an AltGr key because that was relevant to only non-U.S. markets; they simply had "left" and "right" Alt keys.

Reference: (https://blogs.msdn.microsoft.com/oldnewthing/20040329-00/?p=40003/)

128.

Prisoners in Greenland have their cell keys as it's regarded as a sign of privacy and can leave their cell from 6:30AM to 9:30PM.

Reference: (https://en.wikipedia.org/wiki/Law_enforcement_in_Greenland)

129.

Whitney Houston produced the 2001 comedy film "The Princess Diaries."

Reference: (https://en.wikipedia.org/wiki/The_Princess_Diaries_(film))

130.

The world's oldest pool of water was found 2 miles down a Canadian mineshaft and dated at about 2 billion years old. By observing the sulphate in the water, researchers were also able to confirm that single-celled organisms had inhabited the pool at some point.

Reference: (http://www.bbc.com/news/science-environment-38311781)

131.

No symphony orchestra can ever make a profit on its own, even if it sold out tickets at every show. This is mainly because the show consists of 40 to 100 fully salaried members who only perform the same piece 2 or 3 times. Most orchestras rely heavily on donators to be profitable.

Reference: (http://abc.net.au/news/2017-04-04/why-no-symphony-orchestra-in-the-world-makes-money/8413746?pfmredir=sm)

132.

Mike Patton, the frontman of Faith No More and Mr. Bungle, voiced the male infected in the video game Left 4 Dead and GLaDOS's Anger Core in the Portal video game.

Reference: (http://combineoverwiki.net/wiki/Mike_Patton)

133.

The Pitcairn Islands have tried to attract immigrants, but so far none have formally applied. The requirements are: cannot take local jobs, must build your own house but continued residency after 2 years is not guaranteed, must do unpaid roadwork and toilet cleaning, and cannot bring kids under the age of 16.

Reference: (https://en.wikipedia.org/wiki/Pitcairn_Islands#Potential_extinction)

134.

J.K. Rowling, the Harry Potter author, is the second billionaire ever to fall off the Forbes billionaire list because of charitable giving.

Reference: (https://www.snopes.com/j-k-rowling-drops-off-forbes-billionaires-list/)

135.

Ted Nugent for a month stopped bathing, vomited on himself, and defecated in his pants to get out of being drafted during Vietnam.

Reference: (https://www.huffingtonpost.com/2013/01/24/dee-snider-reminds-republicans-ted-nugent-dodged-vietnam-draft_n_2544864.html)

136.

Around 0.5% of the global population lives on Earth's largest tectonic plate.

Reference: (https://en.wikipedia.org/wiki/Pacific_Plate)

137.

Satellites travel at speeds in excess of 17,000 miles per hour.

Reference: (http://science.nationalgeographic.com/science/space/solar-system/orbital/)

138.

On St. Agnes Day, for good luck, girls were told to pray to St. Valentine with their legs crossed.

Reference: (https://www.nature.com/articles/121227a0.pdf)

139.

Kentucky has 120 counties because the rule in the early 1800's was that you needed to be a day rides by horse to the county seat to take care of business.

Reference: (https://www.sos.ky.gov/admin/land/resources/articles/Documents/Counties.pdf)

140.

Some fathers give a "push present", usually jewelry, to the mother of their child immediately following the birth of their baby.

Reference: (https://en.wikipedia.org/wiki/Push_present)

141.

So as not to break the conventions of war, Japan tried to end peace negotiations by sending the United States a letter 30 minutes prior to the attack at Pearl Harbor. Because it took time to transcribe the letter, it was delayed, making the attack a war crime.

Reference: (http://interesting-facts.com/pearl-harbor-facts/#if5)

142.

When Bill Gates made a program to schedule students' classes in his school, he modified the program to put himself in classes with a disproportionate number of interesting girls.

Reference: (https://en.wikipedia.org/wiki/Bill_Gates#Early_life)

143.

The "Concave Hollow Earth" theory states that the Earth is actually the outer edge of a sphere with the entire universe inside it. The theory may eventually have influenced Adolf Hitler.

Reference: (https://en.wikipedia.org/wiki/Hollow_Earth#Concave_Hollow_Earths)

144.

The Japanese believe that blood type influences personality.

Reference: (http://www.issendai.com/rpgs/takemywings/bloodtypes.htm)

145.

Duran Duran's "A View to a Kill" is the only James Bond theme song to reach number 1 on the Billboard Hot 100.

Reference: (https://en.wikipedia.org/wiki/A_View_to_a_Kill_(song))

146.

Marvel's first African hero was Waku, Prince of the Banthu, who predated the Black Panther by almost a dozen years.

Reference: (https://en.wikipedia.org/wiki/Jungle_Action)

147.

The BBC used the opening bars of Beethoven's Fifth Symphony during World War II because it simulated the Morse Code "V" for Victory.

Reference: (https://en.wikipedia.org/wiki/V_sign)

148.

In 1914, Henry Ford published an anti-smoking book that was targeted at young people, years before smoking was widely considered unhealthy.

Reference:(https://en.wikipedia.org/w/index.php?title=Henry_Ford&mobileaction=toggle_view_desktop#Personal_interests)

149.

The Parthenon was largely destroyed by a gun powder explosion in 1687, and not by normal decay.

Reference: (https://en.wikipedia.org/wiki/Parthenon#Destruction)

150.

One of the only top executives to be imprisoned for the Volkswagen Emissions scandal was arrested due to a fluke. Having been transferred back to Germany, he came to the United States for a vacation with his wife and was seized as he waited for a departing flight in Miami.

Reference: (https://www.nytimes.com/2017/12/06/business/oliver-schmidt-volkswagen.html)

151.

When 19th century astronomers Pierre Jules César Janssen and Joseph Norman Lockyer analyzed the spectrum of the Sun through a prism, they observed a bright yellow line which was later concluded to be there due to an "extraterrestrial" element. This element would be later be named helium.

Reference: (https://www.wired.com/2009/08/dayintech-0818/)

152.

Dr. Strangelove was based on a book called Red Alert, which wasn't funny and didn't contain a character named Dr. Strangelove.

Reference: (https://en.wikipedia.org/wiki/Red_Alert_(novel))

153.

Pineapple is the only known source in nature of the enzyme bromelain. Bromelain actually digests proteins, so when you eat a pineapple, it's essentially eating you back.

Reference: (http://www.iflscience.com/plants-and-animals/why-does-eating-pineapple-make-your-mouth-sore)

154.

The NHL uses frozen hockey pucks for all its games so the pucks aren't too bouncy, and the pucks, which are replaced before every period, are kept in a freezer in the penalty box.

Reference: (https://knowledgestew.com/2016/08/hockey-pucks-frozen-nhl.html)

155.

In the winter of 1974, Werner Herzog, on hearing the news his friend Lotte Eisner was gravely ill, took a jacket, compass and a bag of bare essentials and walked from Munich to Paris in an act of faith believing it would save her life.

Reference: (https://en.wikipedia.org/wiki/Of_Walking_in_Ice)

156.

David Hasselhoff kept a 14 foot replica of himself from the SpongeBob SquarePants Movie.

Reference: (http://www.ecanadanow.com/david-hasselhoff-withdraws-auction-lifelike-model-cant-part-with-it/82794/)

157.

Rhythm Tengoku, Japan's original rhythm heaven, had an arcade port from SEGA.

Reference: (https://www.youtube.com/watch?v=1irN4m527kQ)

158.

In 1994, Mark Messier confronted the New York media and publicly guaranteed a Game 6 victory. He backed it up by scoring a natural hat trick in the third period on an empty net goal with ESPN commentator Gary Thorne boasting, "Do you believe it?! Do you believe it?"

Reference: (https://www.youtube.com/watch?v=Uc-pxygcRi8)

159.

There is no generally accepted term to describe what Northern Ireland is: province, region, country or "something else".

Reference: (https://en.wikipedia.org/wiki/Northern_Ireland#descriptions)

160.

The highly radioactive metal, Copernicium, could be a gas at STP.

Reference: (https://en.wikipedia.org/wiki/Copernicium#Physical_and_atomic)

161.

Axl Rose wanted Nirvana to open for the Guns N' Roses and Metallica tour in 1992.

Reference: (http://www.rollingstone.com/music/news/guns-n-roses-vs-nirvana-a-beef-history-20160411)

162.

Former Irish International, Tony Cascarino, joined Gillingham in 1982 for a transfer fee made up of tracksuits and training equipment.

Reference: (https://en.wikipedia.org/wiki/Tony_Cascarino)

163.

The Angonoka tortoise is the most endangered tortoise in the world. Found only around the Baly Bay in Northwest Madagascar, this tortoise, known for distinctive, beautifully decorated carapace, has been suffering from habitat destruction and over-hunting.

Reference: (http://www.iucnredlist.org/details/9016/0)

164.

Eddie Murphy sings reggae music.

Reference: (https://www.youtube.com/watch?v=cJsudoY8vGk)

165.

Eduardo Guerra Jimenez flew a hijacked MiG-17 from Cuba to Miami and defecated to the United States in October, 1969. Almost ten years later, in June, 1979, he hijacked a Delta passenger jet and defected back to Cuba.

Reference: (https://en.wikipedia.org/wiki/List_of_Cold_War_pilot_defections#Cuba)

166.

Comedian Don Rickles co-hosted for Johnny Carson in 1976, during which Rickles broke a cigarette box that Carson had had on his desk for 9 years. When told about it during the next show, Carson tracked down Rickles, who was filming a sitcom in the TV studio next door, and barged in on him.

Reference: (https://heavy.com/entertainment/2017/04/watch-don-rickles-johnny-carson-cigarette-box-bit-incident-cpo-sharkey-tonight-show-original-clip-video-youtube/)

167.

Heroin was synthesized in 1897 at Bayer Pharmaceutical by German chemists looking for a less potent form of morphine. Bayer marketed heroin as a, "non-addictive morphine substitute", for cough suppressants.

Reference: (https://en.wikipedia.org/wiki/Heroin#History)

168.

The runner-up in the 1900 Olympic marathon was ironically named, Emile Champion.

Reference: (https://en.wikipedia.org/wiki/%C3%89mile_Champion)

169.

"Where do you go to my lovely," by Peter Sarstedt refers not to Sophia Loren but his ex-wife Anita Atke.

Reference: (http://www.steynonline.com/5675/where-do-you-go-to-my-lovely)

170.

Hitler had only one testicle.

Reference: (http://www.independent.co.uk/news/world/europe/hitler-only-had-one-testicle-german-historian-claims-a6779481.html)

171.

"Emordnilap" is a word that when spelled backwards produces another word, and therefore "emordnilap palindrome" is a palindrome.

Reference: (https://www.snopes.com/language/apocryph/emordnilap.asp)

172.

A man in Canada smuggled Trader Joe's branded groceries from the United States to sell in his store "Pirate Joes" in Canada.

Reference: (http://www.cbsnews.com/news/pirate-joe-raids-trader-joes-shelves/)

173.

Director Frank Capra graduated from Caltech with a B.S. in chemical engineering. Unable to find work in chemical engineering, he got his first directing role in San Francisco by lying that he had just arrived from Hollywood.

Reference: (https://en.wikipedia.org/wiki/Frank_Capra)

174.

Oasis was once so popular in Britain that a single was released consisting entirely of the Gallagher brothers arguing during an interview, and the single hit number 52 on the U.K. charts.

Reference: (https://en.wikipedia.org/wiki/Wibbling_Rivalry)

175.

Olympic figure skating had a rule that required female competitors to wear skirts and pants. It was called the Katarina Rule.

Reference: (http://www.bbc.com/sport/winter-olympics/43111011)

176.

Our urge to breathe isn't because of our need for oxygen, but our body wanting to get rid of carbon dioxide.

Reference: (http://thedivingblog.com/urge-to-breath/)

177.

A wanted robber known as "Roofman" created a secret hideout inside a Toys R' Us. He played with toys, watched DVDs, ate baby food and installed a baby video monitor to keep an eye on the store.

Reference: (http://www.sfgate.com/news/article/Escaped-robber-returns-to-annals-of-weird-crime-2706176.php)

178.

Willy Wonka's, "We are the music makers...", line is from a 19th century poem.

Reference: (https://en.wikipedia.org/wiki/Ode_(poem))

179.

During the American Civil War, about 56,000 soldiers died as prisoners of war, accounting for almost 10% of all Civil War fatalities.

Reference: (https://en.wikipedia.org/wiki/American_Civil_War_prison_camps)

180.

A mysterious baseball was found in the antenna of Tokyo Tower.

Reference: (http://news.asiaone.com/News/Latest+News/Relax/Story/A1Story20121225-391520.html)

181.

Debi Thomas is arguably the best African American figure skater. He became a medical doctor and is presently bankrupt and living in a trailer.

Reference: (https://www.washingtonpost.com/local/social-issues/the-mystery-of-why-the-best-african-american-figure-skater-in-history-went-bankrupt-and-lives-in-a-trailer/2016/02/25/a191972c-ce99-11e5-abc9-ea152f0b9561_story.html)

182.

Tom Hanks doesn't voice Woody in video games or toys, but rather his brother Jim.

Reference: (https://www.youtube.com/watch?v=LNptl7bjRhI)

183.

In the film Jumanji, the characters of Samuel Parrish, Alan's father, and the hunter Van Pelt, who pursues Alan both in the game world and the real world, are portrayed by the same actor.

Reference: (https://en.wikipedia.org/wiki/Jumanji#Cast)

184.

Buzz Aldrin punched a moon landing denier, Bart Sibrel, in the jaw after Aldrin was tricked into believing that he would be appearing on a Japanese children's television show. Sibrel had brought a film crew to record Aldrin swearing on the Bible that the moon landing wasn't faked.

Reference: (https://en.wikipedia.org/wiki/Buzz_Aldrin)

185.

Helen Keller was a radical Socialist who detested Capitalism as "an intolerable system" that causes blindness and deafness.

Reference:(https://en.wikipedia.org/w/index.php?title=Helen_Keller&mobileaction=toggle_view_desktop#Political_activities)

186.

Galérie des Machines is a glass and steel exhibition hall that covered 20 acres. Rising to a height of 158 feet, the hall was void of internal supports. Completed in 1889, it was demolished in 1910.

Reference: (http://atlasofplaces.com/Galerie-des-Machines-Ferdinand-Dutert)

187.

The unofficial title for Queen Elizabeth II in British Columbia, Canada is "Mother of All People".

Reference: (https://en.wikipedia.org/wiki/List_of_titles_and_honours_of_Queen_Elizabeth_II)

188.

Great Britain is "Great" because Brittany is "Lesser Britain."

Reference: (https://en.wikipedia.org/wiki/Brittany)

189.

In 2015, a fire broke out at a sea park in Taiwan, injuring over 500 people.

Reference: (https://www.yahoo.com/news/fire-injures-scores-attending-party-taiwan-water-park-163921242.html?ref=gs)

190.

In Vito Acconci's 1972 art performance called "Seedbed", he built a hidden chamber under the floor of an exhibit room where he masturbated and spoke his sexual fantasies to the visitors walking above him through a speaker.

Reference: (https://www.metmuseum.org/art/collection/search/266876)

191.

Bamboo is the fastest growing plant in the world and can grow roughly 0.9 meters in a day if presented with the appropriate conditions.

Reference: (http://www.softschools.com/facts/plants/bamboo_facts/563/)

192.

ReCAPTCHAs are used to digitize books. It has already completed digitizing the archives of The New York Times, where more than 13 million articles in total have been archived, dating from 1851 to the present day.

Reference: (https://en.wikipedia.org/wiki/ReCAPTCHA)

193.

There were vampire concentration camps that were used by Germans in World War II to drain Slavic children of their blood.

Reference: (http://exilpen.net/neuigkeiten/texte_neu/texte-der-nicht-mitglieder/vampire.html)

194.

There is a species of spider where the mother commits suicide by allowing her offspring to eat 95% of her 2 weeks after birth. They leave her heart and exoskeleton.

Reference: (https://entomologytoday.org/2015/03/27/arachnid-matriphagy-these-spider-mothers-literally-die-for-their-young/)

195.

Scientists have identified a gene-encoded enzyme in some birds which helps them convert yellow pigments obtained from the diet into red pigments, and then birds use these pigments to color their bills, feathers, and bare skin.

Reference: (http://www.doonwire.com/news/studies-reveal-how-birds-became-red-000027)

196.

Running a stop sign in a commercial or privately owned parking lot is not a violation of law or enforceable by police.

Reference: (http://patch.com/california/sanbruno/ask-a-cop-can-i-get-arrested-for-ignoring-traffic-signs-in-a-mall-parking-lot_2bf3d873)

197.

Building new freeways and widening roads actually increases traffic congestion.

Reference: (http://www.wired.com/2014/06/wuwt-traffic-induced-demand/)

198.

Milhouse from the Simpsons was first created for a Butterfinger chocolate bar commercial.

Reference: (https://en.wikipedia.org/wiki/Milhouse_Van_Houten#Creation)

199.

Schnitzler syndrome is a rare disease that makes the body think it's infected and has symptoms like fever and weight loss.

Reference: (https://en.wikipedia.org/wiki/Schnitzler_syndrome)

200.

Abraham Lincoln refused a case because he believed that some things that are legally right aren't morally right.

Reference: (http://www.abrahamlincolnsclassroom.org/abraham-lincoln-in-depth/abraham-lincoln-and-the-law/)

201.

There is a species of fish that can travel outside of water and breathe air.

Reference: (https://en.wikipedia.org/wiki/Walking_catfish)

202.

Hippos don't swim, they just walk underwater.

Reference: (https://indianapublicmedia.org/amomentofscience/do-hippos-swim/)

203.

The apples in the phrase, "how do you like them apples", refer to World War I trench mortars nicknamed "toffee apples" used by the British.

Reference: (https://en.wikipedia.org/wiki/2-inch_medium_mortar)

204.

The term "lucid dream" was coined by Dutch author and psychiatrist, Frederik van Eeden, in his 1913 article "A Study of Dreams."

Reference: (https://en.wikipedia.org/wiki/Lucid_dream)

205.

A wealthy Canadian lawyer gave $9 million dollars to the mother who had the most children in the Toronto area in the 10 years after his death.

Reference: (http://fivethirtyeight.com/features/how-a-dead-millionaire-convinced-dozens-of-women-to-have-as-many-babies-as-possible/)

206.

The phrase, "Low Man on the Totem Pole", has come to mean the opposite of what it should; the "Low Man" on the totem pole was often the most talented and valuable part of the totem pole creation process.

Reference: (http://users.imag.net/~sry.jkramer/nativetotems/lowman.htm)

207.

In the Vatican Radio Lawsuit, the Vatican Radio Station, outside of Italian jurisdiction, generated electromagnetic fields above Italy's legal limit. A nearby town claimed it had caused higher incidence of child leukemia among other diseases.

Reference: (https://academic.oup.com/aje/article/155/12/1096/123184)

208.

Hitler visited a Canadian War Memorial in France after capturing the region and chose not to destroy it, as he admired its peacefulness.

Reference:(https://en.wikipedia.org/wiki/Canadian_National_Vimy_Memorial#Second_World_War)

209.

Jean-Paul Sartre hallucinated crabs his whole life.

Reference: (http://www.critical-theory.com/9-insane-stories-from-the-lives-of-famous-existentialists/)

210.

The Heavy Falcon was eclipsed in size by the Sea Dragon, a floating space-race era rocket that was designed to be floated out to sea and launched from beneath the water.

Reference: (https://www.youtube.com/watch?v=yiTjbsiKu6g&ab_channel=VintageSpace)

211.

Air India have crashed twice on the same mountain, Mont Blanc. About 50 years later, the glacier on the mountain is melting and giving up aircraft and human parts.

Reference: (https://en.wikipedia.org/wiki/Air_India_Flight_245)

212.

A company created a small speaker which a pregnant mother can insert into her vagina so that her unborn baby can listen to music.

Reference: (https://www.youtube.com/watch?v=JAsIx2gSsWA&feature=youtu.be)

213.

Paul Verhoeven, the director of "Robocop" and "Total Recall" never read the book "Starship Troopers" before making a movie based on it because he found it "boring."

Reference: (https://en.wikipedia.org/wiki/Starship_Troopers_%28film%29)

214.

Curry Haynes was awarded ten Purple Hearts during his service in the Vietnam War, the most in U.S. Military history. Nine of them were earned in a single day.

Reference: (http://onlineathens.com/local-news-mobile/2015-10-17/vietnam-veteran-10-purple-heart-awards-recalls-violent-battle)

215.

Zheleznogorsk, a limited-access Russian town originally built for producing weapons-grade plutonium, has a city flag which portrays a bear splitting an atom apart.

216.

Multicellular life is already more than 2 billion years old.

Reference: (https://en.wikipedia.org/wiki/Francevillian_biota)

217.

Piezoelectricity, the electric energy exerted from crystals under stress, has been shown to significantly increase successful fertilization in completely infertile couples when paired with standard sperm injection procedures.

Reference: (http://www.omicsonline.org/open-access/the-effect-of-piezoelectric-stimulation-in-patients-with-low-fertilization-potential-2161-0436.1000122.pdf)

218.

The entire population of Earth lives on just 1% of the land.

Reference: (http://metrocosm.com/world-population-split-in-half-map/)

219.

The word Yosemite, which is derived from a Southern Miwok word "Yehemite" and which translates to, "Some among them are killers," is believed to be how Mariposa-area native peoples referred to the people who lived in Yosemite Valley.

Reference: (https://www.yosemitethisyear.com/faq)

220.

The United States is ranked 14th in the world for percentage of the population which are English speakers.

Reference: (https://en.wikipedia.org/wiki/List_of_countries_by_English-speaking_population)

221.

Certain parts of the world call all sodas "Coke."

Reference: (https://en.wikipedia.org/wiki/Names_for_soft_drinks_in_the_United_States)

222.

In 2017, the Motion Picture Academy invited 774 new members into their group of over 7,000 voting members. 39% of them were women. That alone was an increase of 359% of female invitees over the previous two years.

Reference: (https://thescene.com/watch/vanityfair/15-actors-who-were-recently-invited-to-the-academy)

223.

In the "Queengate" cover-up at Memorial High School in Eau Claire, Wisconsin, a 17 year old girl was voted homecoming queen but had her ballots burned due to being pregnant. The eventual investigation led to the resigning of the school's principal.

Reference:(https://en.wikipedia.org/wiki/Memorial_High_School_(Eau_Claire,_Wisconsin)#Homecoming_election_scandal)

224.

The banana tree is actually not a tree but the world's largest herb.

Reference: (http://dontwastethecrumbs.com/2012/09/the-benefits-and-frugality-of-the-worlds-largest-herb-the-banana/)

225.

A form of HD VHS called "D-VHS" was released in 1998.

Reference: (https://en.wikipedia.org/wiki/D-VHS)

226.

The $3 Presidential Election Campaign Fund now goes to the NIH for pediatric research.

Reference: (https://en.wikipedia.org/wiki/Gabriella_Miller_Kids_First_Research_Act)

227.

The House of Representatives has a tutorial on how to write legislation.

Reference: (https://legcounsel.house.gov/HOLC/Drafting_Legislation/Drafting_Guide.html#I)

228.

Charles Darwin had a penchant for eating exotic animals.

Reference: (http://io9.gizmodo.com/what-did-charles-darwin-put-in-his-mouth-pretty-much-e-1687788345)

229.

Three Alcatraz escapees used fake heads of plaster, paint and human hair in their beds to fool night guards. They then made a drill using a vacuum motor to loosen air vents, built a raft from over 50 raincoats, paddles with a musical instrument, and a fake bolt made from soap to close their escape hatch.

Reference: (https://www.fbi.gov/news/stories/2007/june/alcatraz_060807)

230.

Then 13 year-old Danielle Lei, a Girl Scout in San Francisco, was the first Girl Scout to make news by selling cookies outside a marijuana dispensary. She sold 117 boxes in 2 hours.

Reference: (http://www.latimes.com/food/dailydish/la-dd-girl-scout-sells-cookies-pot-clinic-20140221-story.html)

231.

Taiwan had plans to invade and retake mainland China, post-Civil War. It was led by the first President of the ROC Chiang Kai-shek. Kai-shek effectively geared up the nation for a recapture of the mainland, but was cancelled in 1972 after numerous failures with deaths and active U.S. opposition.

Reference: (https://en.wikipedia.org/wiki/Project_National_Glory)

232.

The expression "skin of my teeth" originates from the Bible in Job 19:20.

Reference: (https://en.wikipedia.org/wiki/Skin_of_my_teeth)

233.

Your body could be attacked by the new cells in a bone marrow transplant and it can cause chronic issues.

Reference: (https://www.nlm.nih.gov/medlineplus/ency/article/001309.htm)

234.

The Library of Congress contains a book written in Emoji called "Emoji Dick".

Reference:(https://catalog.loc.gov/vwebv/search?searchCode=LCCN&searchArg=2012454709&searchType=1&permalink=y)

235.

In 1942, Disney made a training film to teach Canadian soldiers on how to operate a Boys Mk1, which was an anti-tank rifle.

Reference: (https://en.wikipedia.org/wiki/Stop_That_Tank!)

236.

In 1918, the geographic center of the United States was determined by balancing a cardboard cutout shape of the United States on a point. It was accurate to within 20 miles.

Reference: (https://en.wikipedia.org/wiki/Geographic_center_of_the_contiguous_United_States#Method_of_measurement)

237.

The term "Third World" originated in the Cold War era and refers to the neutral status of nations not directly allied to either NATO or the communist bloc. It is therefore not a financial classification for poor nations.

Reference: (https://en.wikipedia.org/wiki/Third_World)

238.

Bill Nye's father was working as a contractor on Wake Island when it was captured by the Japanese on December 8, 1941, and spent the war as a prisoner of war. He spent time making sundials using a shovel to pass the time.

Reference: (https://www.huffingtonpost.com/entry/bill-nye-pearl-harbor-father_us_584885cee4b0641041459066)

239.

When the First World War began, it was compulsory for all British officers to have a moustache. Poignantly, that edict was revoked in October, 1916, because the new recruits were so young that some could not grow more than a thin, mousey streak.

Reference: (http://www.telegraph.co.uk/news/features/3634260/How-the-moustache-went-the-way-of-the-British-Empire.html)

240.

The United States developed a plane in 1955 with a supersonic propeller capable of knocking people over, causing nausea, headaches and even seizures.

Reference: (https://en.wikipedia.org/wiki/Republic_XF-84H#Noise)

241.

The rock band "Pixies" were offered to compose a song for the Shrek 2 soundtrack, but it was later refused.

Reference: (https://en.wikipedia.org/wiki/Joey_Santiago#Pixies_reunion_and_future_projects)

242.

The world's oldest wine is 1630 years old. It was unearthed at a Roman tomb in Germany.

Reference: (https://en.wikipedia.org/wiki/Speyer_wine_bottle)

243.

Some cows in France are given 2 bottles worth of wine to drink every day, and apparently the resulting beef is delicious.

Reference: (http://newsfeed.time.com/2012/07/14/loaded-livestock-french-farmers-serve-cows-two-bottles-of-wine-per-day/)

244.

Thomson and other airlines use smells like sun cream in their air freshener to entice customers to arrange vacations while they're there.

Reference: (http://www.travelagentcentral.com/trends-research/using-smells-sell-vacations-16018)

245.

There is a widespread but incorrect belief that onscreen portrayals of U.S. Military uniforms must contain inaccuracies to protect actors and producers against claims of impersonating military forces.

Reference: (http://www.myservicepride.com/content/hollywood-make-mistakes-movie-awards/)

246.

Robert Rodriguez and John Malkovich made a movie and put it in a time capsule only to be released in 100 years.

Reference: (https://www.hollywoodreporter.com/news/john-malkovich-robert-rodriguez-movie-hundred-100-years-842692)

247.

The world's highest major city is El Alto, Bolivia, with an elevation of 13,615 feet, or 4,150 meters.

Reference: (https://en.wikipedia.org/wiki/El_Alto)

248.

A stowaway Greek cat flew in the undercarriage of an Airbus A321 from Athens to Zurich, had shock and hypothermia, but survived.

Reference: (http://www.thelocal.ch/20130802/stowaway-cat-survives-flight-from-athens)

249.

DC shoes offered the city of Philadelphia $1 million dollars to unban skateboarding at Love Park.

Reference: (http://articles.philly.com/2011-02-28/news/28637644_1_love-park-skateboarding-ban-dc-shoes)

250.

The stuffed walrus at the Horniman Museum in London is nearly spherical because the people who stuffed it over 100 years ago had almost certainly never seen a real walrus, or an image of one, so they probably just kept stuffing it until it was "full".

Reference: (https://www.horniman.ac.uk/index.php/collections/browse-our-collections/object/190371)

251.

Toussaint Louverture, the man responsible for ensuring Haiti became a free and independent country, never got to be the leader as he died in armed conflict.

Reference: (https://en.wikipedia.org/wiki/Toussaint_Louverture)

252.

William Bullock invented the web rotary printing press. Several years after its invention, his foot was crushed during the installation of a new machine in Philadelphia. The crushed foot developed gangrene and Bullock died during the amputation.

Reference: (http://news.discovery.com/human/life/inventors-killed-by-inventions-101001.htm)

253.

The Basque people dominated the whaling industry in Europe for 500 years and were described as "the only people who understand whaling," by British explorer Jonas Poole.

Reference: (https://en.wikipedia.org/wiki/History_of_Basque_whaling#cite_note-MarBarkBark2003-1)

254.

Madrid has the oldest running restaurant in the world named Sobrino de Botín which hasn't closed its doors once since its founding in 1725.

Reference: (https://en.wikipedia.org/wiki/Sobrino_de_Bot%C3%ADn)

255.

Up until 2016, there was a law in Paris that required local bakeries to spread out their vacation time so that there was enough bread for the city during the holidays.

Reference: (https://www.cnbc.com/2017/08/25/vacation-can-make-you-more-productive--just-ask-the-europeans.html)

256.

Uma Thurman, Patrick Stewart, Shia Labouf and Mark Hamill's voices all appear in the English dub of Nausicaa of the Valley of the Wind.

Reference: (https://www.youtube.com/watch?v=RnNhsD_Q0Rw)

257.

The International Space Station is arguably the most expensive single item ever constructed. In 2010, the cost was expected to be $150 billion. Assuming 20,000 person-days of use from 2000 to 2015 by two to six person crews, each person-day would cost $7.5 million dollars.

Reference: (https://en.wikipedia.org/wiki/International_Space_Station#Cost)

258.

A lonely little tree found a home on a log sticking out of Fairy Lake in British Columbia.

Reference: (https://www.atlasobscura.com/places/the-tree-on-the-lake)

259.

After legal objections to Sherlock Holmes appearing in his Arsène Lupin series, Leblanc simply renamed him "Herlock Sholmes".

Reference:(https://en.wikipedia.org/wiki/Ars%C3%A8ne_Lupin#Ars%C3%A8ne_Lupin_and_Sherlock_Holmes)

260.

In 1903, William Nelson, a General Electric employee, invented a new way to motorize bicycles. He then fell off his prototype bike during a test run and died as a result of his injuries.

Reference: (http://mentalfloss.com/article/48723/6-inventors-killed-their-own-inventions)

261.

The child from The Shinning, Danny Lloyd, stopped acting as he grew up and went on to become a professor of biology.

Reference: (http://nydailynews.com/entertainment/boy-shining-pig-farmer-science-teacher-article-1.1477838)

262.

700 Canadian soldiers are credited with keeping an entire Chinese division, a reoccupation force, from taking Seoul during the Korean War.

Reference: (http://nationalpost.com/news/canada/korean-war-battle-of-kapyong-among-canadas-greatest-victories)

263.

On June 26th, 2014, the owner of Matt's Bar, located in Minneapolis, Minnesota, who claims to have created the infamous Jucy Lucy, died hours before the former president of the United States was scheduled to visit.

Reference: (https://en.wikipedia.org/wiki/Matt's_Bar)

264.

Donkey milk is similar to human breast milk, and was used as a substitute until the beginning of the 20th century.

Reference: (https://www.youtube.com/watch?v=a7sKTEabsb4&feature=youtu.be&t=63)

265.

Farmed salmon is naturally gray in color. It ends up pink due to food additive canthaxanthin and astaxanthin.

Reference: (http://www.wired.com/2004/02/the-15-colors-of-salmon/)

266.

The bestselling solo album of any of the members of ABBA is Frida's "Something's Going On" from 1982. The album was produced by Phil Collins and includes a duet with him and Frida.

Reference: (https://en.wikipedia.org/wiki/Something%27s_Going_On)

267.

A "birthgasm" is a female orgasm that occurs during childbirth. This is sometimes referred to as an "orgasmic childbirth."

Reference: (https://en.wikipedia.org/wiki/Birthgasm)

268.

Darren Bray of Barry, Wales, choked to death on a burger that he attempted to eat in one go after a night out drinking with friends.

Reference: (http://www.theguardian.com/uk-news/2016/feb/04/inquest-hears-man-died-after-trying-to-eat-burger-in-one-mouthful)

269.

Prince used the heartbeat of his unborn son as part of the percussion in one track on the "Emancipation" album. By the time the album was released, his son had died of a congenital birth defect.

Reference: (https://en.wikipedia.org/wiki/Emancipation_(Prince_album)#Overview)

270.

Butter sticks that are sold in the United States come in two distinct shapes, although containing the same amount of butter, depending to a large extent on whether it is being sold East or West of the Rocky Mountains.

Reference: (https://en.wikipedia.org/wiki/Butter#Size_and_shape_of_packaging)

271.

Only 20 states have laws requiring breaks for meals.

Reference: (https://www.dol.gov/whd/state/meal2017.htm)

272.

Guinness saved the Irish economy during World War II, when the United Kingdom cut the supply of coal and fertilizer to Ireland because the Irish kept neutral instead of joining the Allies. Later, Ireland cut exports of beers and the army's complaints pushed the United Kingdom to restart exporting wheat, coal and fertilizers in exchange for Guinness.

Reference: (http://www.irishcentral.com/roots/history/How-Guinness-saved-Ireland-in-World-War-II.html)

273.

The Manson Impact Crater in Iowa was once thought to be the impact that killed the dinosaurs, until it was proven to be too old at 74 million years.

Reference: (https://en.wikipedia.org/wiki/Manson_crater)

274.

Snow White and the Seven Dwarfs syncs up with The Beatles' White Album.

Reference: (http://www.moviessynced.com/page2/index.html)

275.

In the summer of 1974, the CIA hatched an audacious plan to salvage a lost Soviet submarine K-129; so they could explore Moscow's nuclear missiles and to break into its naval communications.

Reference: (http://www.bbc.co.uk/news/resources/idt-sh/deep_sea_mining)

276.

Before Michael Bay became famous for movies like Armageddon, Pearl Harbor, and Transformers, he directed music videos for Meatloaf, including "I'd Do Anything for Love" and "Objects in the Rear View Mirror May Appear Closer than They Are."

Reference:(https://en.wikipedia.org/wiki/Rock_and_Roll_Dreams_Come_Through#Music_videos)

277.

According to a study in Poland, attractive people are happier than others but only when they think about their looks.

Reference: (http://sportige.com/beautiful-people-are-happier-only-when-they-think-about-it-92273/)

278.

It was only 10 years ago that LCD TVs first outsold CRT TVs.

Reference: (https://www.engadget.com/2008/02/19/worldwide-lcd-tv-shipments-surpass-crts-for-first-time-ever/)

279.

Christian Dominionism seeks to put Christians in governmental positions so they could impose Biblical laws.

Reference: (https://en.wikipedia.org/wiki/Dominion_theology)

280.

Pink Floyd's early success was propelled by an economics lecturer who helped them get positive coverage in the U.K.'s Financial Times newspaper.

Reference: (https://en.wikipedia.org/wiki/Pink_Floyd)

281.

According to VISA, the average American household with teenagers spent $324 on "promposing," otherwise known as asking someone to prom.

282.

There's an English word for the sound of the wind in the trees. The word is "psithurism".

Reference: (https://www.wordnik.com/words/psithurism)

283.

The word with the most meanings in English is the verb "set", with 430 senses listed in the Second Edition of the Oxford English Dictionary, published in 1989. The word commands the longest entry in the dictionary at 60,000 words, or 326,000 characters.

Reference: (https://www.thespruce.com/which-word-has-the-most-definitions-4077796)

284.

For many years, the Sultans of the Ottoman Empire would execute siblings who could compete for the throne.

Reference: (http://www.ekrembugraekinci.com/makale.asp?id=615)

285.

A pub in Dublin had a strike that lasted fourteen years.

Reference: (https://comeheretome.com/2012/01/02/the-dublin-strike-that-lasted-fourteen-years/)

286.

The rapper Drake owns a pair of solid gold OVO Air Jordan 10s, made by artist Matthew Senna. According to the owner, the shoes weigh about 100 pounds.

Reference: (http://www.esquire.com/style/news/a46795/drake-gold-jordans/)

287.

In 363 AD, an earthquake destroyed much of Petra, and crippled the vital water management system. The last inhabitants abandoned the city after it was further weakened by another major earthquake in 551 AD.

Reference: (https://www.svrf.com/vr/The-Ancient-World/84748)

288.

The movie "The China Syndrome" came out on March 16th, 1979. 12 days later, the Three Mile Island nuclear accident happened.

Reference: (https://en.wikipedia.org/wiki/The_China_Syndrome)

289.

95 year old Li Xiufeng spent 6 days inside a coffin after her neighbor assumed that she had died in her sleep after failing to wake her up. On the day before her funeral, her neighbors were stunned when they saw that the coffin was empty. Afterwards, they found her in the kitchen cooking.

Reference: (http://www.mirror.co.uk/news/weird-news/zombie-gran-95-year-old-chinese-woman-746295)

290.

Love at first sight has some scientific evidence.

Reference: (https://en.wikipedia.org/wiki/Love_at_first_sight#Psychological_conceptions)

291.

When LeBron James left Cleveland for Miami, sports-memorabilia company Fathead lowered the price of wall graphics depicting James from $99.99 to $17.41, the birth year of Benedict Arnold.

Reference: (https://nesn.com/2010/07/cavs-owner-dan-gilbert-changes-price-of-lebron-james-fatheads-to-benedict-arnolds-birth-year/)

292.

In 1975, an American businessman named Robert Macauley chartered a Boeing 747 and arranged for 300 orphaned Vietnamese children to leave the country, paying for the trip by mortgaging his house.

Reference: (https://en.wikipedia.org/wiki/Robert_Macauley)

293.

The creator of the National Enquirer, Generoso Pope Jr., worked for the CIA's psychological warfare unit.

Reference: (https://en.wikipedia.org/wiki/Generoso_Pope,_Jr.)

294.

"Stupider" is grammatically correct.

Reference: (https://www.grammarly.com/blog/is-stupider-a-word/)

295.

Slang terms for vaginal flatulence include vart, queef, and fanny fart.

Reference: (https://en.wikipedia.org/wiki/Vaginal_flatulence)

296.

Paul Anderson's feat of lifting 6,270 pounds with his back was recorded in the 1985 edition of the Guinness Book of World Records as, "the greatest weight ever raised by a human being."

Reference: (http://www.newyorker.com/books/double-take/paul-anderson-worlds-strongest-man)

297.

Looting of DJ equipment during the 1977 New York City blackout contributed to the rise of hip-hop.

Reference: (https://en.wikipedia.org/wiki/New_York_City_blackout_of_1977)

298.

The sugar industry promoted sugar as a weight loss product.

Reference: (http://www.businessinsider.com/vintage-sugar-as-diet-aid-ads-2014-10?international=true&r=US&IR=T)

299.

In 2015, Americans left 658 million vacation days unused. 222 million of those days were lost because they could not be rolled over, meaning Americans worked $61 billion worth of time for free.

Reference: (http://www.smh.com.au/business/workplace-relations/why-millennials-dont-take-holidays-20161220-gtf26j.html)

300.

During World War II, the United Sates put out the "Sabotage Field Manual" which described ways that ordinary citizens could sabotage the Nazis by doing things such as, "holding conferences when there is more critical work," and, "issuing 2 train tickets for the same seat to create an argument."

Reference: (https://www.cia.gov/news-information/featured-story-archive/2012-featured-story-archive/simple-sabotage.html)

301.

Stir frying wasn't a common cooking technique in the home in China until the 20th century, when cooking oil and fuel became more affordable.

Reference: (https://en.wikipedia.org/wiki/Stir_frying)

302.

One of the most famous gods of Hinduism, Shiva, is worshiped in the form of a statue of his penis that nearly always rests on a pedestal of a female sex organ.

Reference: (http://www.religionfacts.com/shiva-linga)

303.

In Hallelujah by Leonard Cohen, "the fourth, the fifth, the minor fall, and the major lift" actually refer to the chords the piano is playing at the time.

Reference: (https://www.youtube.com/watch?v=YSlIKe_2kG8)

304.

"Vinegar eels" are microscopic round worms that live in raw unfiltered vinegars such as apple cider vinegars and kombucha.

Reference: (http://www.ripleys.com/blog/the-science-of-vinegar-eels/)

305.

Having a fetish for human hair is called Trchophillia.

Reference: (https://en.wikipedia.org/wiki/Hair_fetishism)

306.

Christina Ricci used to buy cocaine from a place called Kokie's in Brooklyn.

Reference: (http://nuvomagazine.com/magazine/summer-2017/christina-ricci)

307.

Elvis Presley was an identical twin. He had an older twin brother who was sadly stillborn.

Reference: (http://www.thesundayleader.lk/2011/12/25/ten-things-you-didnt-know-about-elvis-presley/)

308.

Universal studios repeatedly requested that the movie "Scarface" be released with a "rap score." De Palma, the director, denied all of the requests because he preferred the original score made by Giorgio Moroder.

Reference: (https://en.wikipedia.org/wiki/Scarface_(1983_film))

Because bullets move faster than sound, a shot to the head could kill you before you even hear the gun fire.

Reference: (https://en.wikipedia.org/wiki/Bullet#Propulsion)

310.

The Monkey's Paw in Toronto has the world's first "Biblio-Mat", a vending machine that will dispense a randomly selected vintage volume for $2.

Reference: (https://www.atlasobscura.com/places/the-monkey-s-paw)

311.

The oldest restaurant in the world is Sobrino de Botín of Madrid, Spain. This has been officiated by the Guinness Book of World Records. The restaurant opened in 1725 which would make it 293 years old.

Reference: (https://en.wikipedia.org/wiki/Sobrino_de_Bot%C3%ADn)

312.

The dark net is known to host a wide range of underground or emergent sub cultures, such as social media racists, self-harm communities, cryptoanarchists and transhumanists.

Reference: (https://en.wikipedia.org/wiki/Darknet)

313.

Santeria Rum is made from a reactor that gives whiskeys and rums many of the qualities of 20 years of barrel aging in less than a week.

Reference: (http://www.montereycountyweekly.com/news/cover/lost-spirits-technology-a-new-way-to-make-superb-liquor/article_5fb58d2e-9ed1-11e5-b15c-dffd4a3ce75f.html)

314.

"Treeman Syndrome" is a rare, incurable disease that sprouts tree-like warts all over the body, and makes hands and feet look like real-life Groot.

Reference: (https://en.wikipedia.org/wiki/Epidermodysplasia_verruciformis)

315.

Caffeine prevents cataracts.

Reference: (https://www.ncbi.nlm.nih.gov/pmc/articles/PMC4734813/#!po=26.8519)

316.

A Tachyon is a hypothetical particle that always moves faster than light.

Reference: (https://en.wikipedia.org/wiki/Tachyon)

317.

Americans are 23% more likely to develop cancer than Mediterranean Europeans.

Reference: (http://publications.cancerresearchuk.org/downloads/product/worldmap.pdf)

318.

Slash created the opening riff for "Sweet Child O' Mine" subconsciously during a casual conversation, and it just so happened to work.

Reference: (https://www.youtube.com/watch?v=_OZMNZCq9WU)

319.

Hashtags, #, used to be called the Octotherp.

Reference: (https://www.gizmodo.com.au/2014/12/before-the-hashtag-there-was-the-octothorpe/)

320.

William Daniels, who plays Mr. Feeny in "Boy Meet's World," is the voice of K.I.T.T. in the 1982 television show "Knight Rider."

Reference: (https://en.wikipedia.org/wiki/William_Daniels)

321.

The Irukandji Jellyfish is a tiny jellyfish whose sting brings feelings of impending doom.

Reference: (https://en.wikipedia.org/wiki/Irukandji_jellyfish#Irukandji_syndrome)

322.

Cleveland kidnapping victim Amanda Berry, held for almost 10 years and freed in 2013, has a TV segment on the Cleveland news dedicated to finding missing people.

Reference: (https://www.today.com/news/cleveland-kidnapping-victim-amanda-berry-has-new-tv-role-helping-t107898)

323.

In racing, there is a very dangerous fire called an "invisible fire." It's caused by methanol igniting. It usually gets all over the pit crew and is very hard to put out because it's so hard to see the flames.

Reference: (https://www.youtube.com/watch?v=MnDX4FpDAzQ&feature=youtu.be)

324.

The last execution by guillotine was in 1977.

Reference: (https://en.wikipedia.org/wiki/Guillotine)

325.

Victoria Secret Bombshell has been shown to be a strong mosquito repellent with effects lasting longer than 120 minutes.

Reference: (http://jinsectscience.oxfordjournals.org/content/15/1/140#F1)

326.

Vintage arcade games need old TVs that use CRT display technology. However, many manufacturers are no longer making CRTs, and the little CRTs that are left are about to sell out.

Reference: (https://venturebeat.com/2017/03/03/what-the-death-of-the-crt-display-technology-means-for-classic-arcade-machines/)

327.

Janet Jackson has a musical sex trilogy with Control's "Let's Wait Awhile," Rhythm Nation's "Someday is Tonight" and 20 Y.O.'s "With You." Together the songs chronicle a woman choosing to wait, then one day deciding to have sex, and finally the romantic confusion after the act of intimacy.

Reference: (https://en.wikipedia.org/wiki/Let%27s_Wait_Awhile)

328.

Vermont is the U.S. state with the highest percentage of people claiming no religion.

Reference: (https://en.wikipedia.org/wiki/Irreligion_in_the_United_States#Tables)

329.

Rolex is a private non-profit company. It's owned by a trust which is run by custodians who do not benefit financially. Rolex profit is either re-invested in the company or donated to charities in Geneva.

Reference: (http://www.rolex.com/watches/rolex-watchmaking.html)

330.

Richard Nixon had the Secret Service uniform redesigned to closely resemble that of European palace guards. The "toy soldier" uniforms were universally ridiculed and only used for a few months before being mothballed; after a decade in storage they were sold to an Iowa high school marching band.

Reference: (http://www.weirduniverse.net/blog/comments/nixon_palace_guard)

331.

A penguin named "Jinjing" swims 5,000 miles every year to visit his rescuer.

Reference: (https://www.youtube.com/watch?v=oks2R4LqWtE)

332.

A 12th century man named "Roland the Farter" received 30 acres of land from King Henry II in exchange for an annual Christmas performance of one jump, one whistle and one fart.

Reference: (https://en.wikipedia.org/wiki/Roland_the_Farter)

333.

Famous naturalist John Audubon made up at least 28 fake species of animals to prank his rival.

Reference: (http://www.atlasobscura.com/articles/audubon-made-up-at-least-28-fake-species-to-prank-a-rival)

334.

Canada Post took 45 years to deliver a letter to sisters that lived 215 kilometers apart.

Reference: (http://nationalpost.com/news/canada/canada-post-takes-45-years-to-deliver-letter-to-calgary-woman-living-just-215-kilometres-away-from-sender)

335.

There is an emergency room in Columbus, Ohio named the "Abercrombie and Fitch Emergency Room".

Reference: (https://www.thelantern.com/2013/09/commentary-abercrombie-fitch-name-poor-choice-ohio-state-emergency-department/)

336.

The "PT" in "PT Cruiser" stands for "Personal Transport."

Reference: (https://en.wikipedia.org/wiki/Chrysler_PT_Cruiser)

337.

Only 30 episodes of Hanna-Barbera's "Top Cat" were made.

Reference: (https://en.wikipedia.org/wiki/Top_Cat)

338.

Clint Eastwood guest starred on "Mister Ed".

Reference: (https://www.youtube.com/watch?v=qGdxxMECZz4&feature=youtu.be)

339.

Sublime made "40oz. to Freedom" by sneaking into the music department at CSU-Dominguez Hills after hours and recording all night.

Reference: (https://en.wikipedia.org/wiki/40oz._to_Freedom)

340.

In 2007, Erika Eiffel, an American woman, "married" the Eiffel Tower.

Reference: (https://en.wikipedia.org/wiki/Eiffel_Tower#In_popular_culture)

341.

Lil Wayne's debut album at age 17 contained almost no explicit lyrics from Wayne himself at his mother's request.

Reference: (https://en.wikipedia.org/wiki/Tha_Block_Is_Hot)

342.

In the early 17th century London, there was a gay brothel on the site where Buckingham Palace is today.

Reference: (http://rictornorton.co.uk/eighteen/molly2.htm)

343.

O.J. Simpson was sued by DirecTV for pirating their signals and had to pay a total of $58,678 for the judgment and attorney fees.

Reference: (https://en.wikipedia.org/wiki/O._J._Simpson#cite_note-88)

344.

In men worldwide, the mean intravaginal ejaculation latency time, defined as "the time between the start of the vaginal intromission and the start of intravaginal ejaculation," is 5.4 minutes.

Reference: (http://www.ncbi.nlm.nih.gov/pubmed/16422843)

345.

In Songdo, South Korea, there are no garbage trucks, instead the household waste is sucked directly from individual kitchens, through a network of underground pipes to waste processing centers.

Reference: (http://www.bbc.co.uk/news/technology-23757738)

346.

Jimi Hendrix pretended to be gay so he would be discharged from the army.

Reference: (http://news.bbc.co.uk/2/hi/entertainment/4730547.stm)

347.

Russia has a territory designated specifically for Jews, established in 1934. Only 0.2% of the population is actually Jewish.

Reference: (https://en.wikipedia.org/wiki/Jewish_Autonomous_Oblast)

348.

The Eiffel Tower has been used for making radio transmissions since the beginning of the 20th century.

Reference: (https://en.wikipedia.org/wiki/Eiffel_Tower#Communications)

349.

In 1985, Ryan White was refused re-entry to his school due to him having AIDS. 117 parents and 50 teachers petitioned for his ban. People even cancelled their subscriptions as White was the paperboy and they believed that they would be infected through the newsprint

Reference: (https://en.wikipedia.org/wiki/Ryan_White#Battle_with_schools)

350.

In 1997, during the STS-96 mission to the ISS, StarCraft became the first video game launched into space.

Reference: (http://us.battle.net/sc2/en/blog/21029405/the-astronaut-who-brought-starcraft-into-space-9-7-2017)

351.

A man once discovered a mole inside the mouth of a large bass.

Reference: (https://www.providr.com/mole-discovered-inside-mouth-of-large-bass/2/)

352.

The original title of "Friends" was going to be "Six of One." Monica was intended for Janeane Garofalo and Courtney Cox was originally offered the role of Rachel.

Reference: (http://abcnews.go.com/blogs/entertainment/2012/04/friends-was-originally-called-six-of-one/)

353.

When cooking certain vegetables in a microwave, minerals in the veggies act like tiny pieces of metal and can create sparks and burns.

Reference: (http://www.inspection.gc.ca/food/information-for-consumers/fact-sheets/specific-products-and-risks/fruits-and-vegetables/sparks-when-cooking/eng/1332278105073/1332278331477)

354.

Madonna, Whitney Houston, Phil Collins and George Michael are tied for the second most number 1 hits in the 1980s with 7 each.

Reference: (https://en.wikipedia.org/wiki/List_of_Billboard_Hot_100_number-one_singles_of_the_1980s)

355.

In World War I, sauerkraut's name in America was changed to liberty cabbage as propaganda against Germany.

Reference: (https://wiktionary.org/wiki/liberty_cabbage)

356.

The longtime boyfriend of Deborah Ann Woll, the actress who plays Karen Page on Marvel's blind super hero show "Daredevil," is blind.

Reference: (http://nypost.com/2015/04/06/daredevil-role-is-personal-for-deborah-ann-woll/)

357.

Apple spends $236 to make each iPhone 6S Plus device, which it sells for over three times that value at $749. Also, a 64 gigabyte iPhone costs Apple about $17 more to make than a 16 gigabyte iPhone, but Apple charges iPhone buyers $100 more for the increased memory.

Reference: (http://www.cnbc.com/2015/09/30/apple-iphone-6s-plus-costs-236-to-make-sells-for-749.html)

358.

Humming the Bee Gees "Staying Alive" keeps the right rhythm when providing CPR compressions on the chest area.

Reference: (https://www.consumerreports.org/first-aid/a-guide-to-smarter-cpr/)

359.

Volkswagen stored its emission-cheating cars at the giant parking lot next to the abandoned Pontiac Silverdome, the former home of the Detroit Lions.

Reference:(http://www.mlive.com/news/detroit/index.ssf/2017/01/vw_silverdome_stash_house.html)

360.

There is a town in northwest Pennsylvania named North East.

Reference: (https://en.wikipedia.org/wiki/North_East,_Pennsylvania)

361.

The U.K. military has a Skynet network, which is a network of satellites which provide strategic communication services to the three branches of the British Armed Forces and NATO forces engaged on coalition tasks.

Reference: (https://en.wikipedia.org/wiki/Skynet_(satellite))

362.

King Abdullah II of Jordan appeared in the Star Trek Voyager episode "Investigations" in a non-speaking role.

Reference: (https://en.wikipedia.org/wiki/Abdullah_II_of_Jordan#Personal_life)

363.

Burger King in Australia is called Hungry Jack's.

Reference: (https://en.wikipedia.org/wiki/Hungry_Jack's)

364.

After Mozart died, Salieri went on to teach. His students included Beethoven, Liszt and Schubert.

Reference: (https://en.wikipedia.org/wiki/Antonio_Salieri#Life_after_opera_.281804.E2.80.9318 25.29)

365.

Dave Grohl tried to quit Nirvana once, after he overheard Kurt Cobain calling him a "shitty drummer," but was convinced to stay by the bands manager.

Reference: (http://www.thestrut.com/2014/04/07/dave-grohl-once-quit-nirvana-after-overhearing-kurt-cobain-call-him-a-shitty-drummer/)

366.

A serial killer appeared on an unaired episode of Bullseye with footage from the show matching him to witness descriptions.

Reference: (https://en.wikipedia.org/wiki/John_Cooper_(serial_killer))

367.

Although it may feel like it, a headache is not actually a pain in your brain. The brain tells you when other parts of your body hurt, but it can't feel pain itself.

Reference: (http://kidshealth.org/en/teens/headaches.html)

368.

When Werner Herzog found out that the monkeys he purchased to be in his movie "Aguirre, the Wrath of God," were being sent to someone else, he pretended to be a veterinarian and stole them back. He loaded all 400 of them into his jeep, used them in the movie and then set them free into the wild.

Reference: (https://en.wikipedia.org/wiki/Aguirre,_the_Wrath_of_God)

369.

Thai Police Officers who are guilty of committing minor transgressions such as coming late or parking at the wrong spot have to wear a bright pink Hello Kitty armband for several days as punishment.

Reference: (http://news.bbc.co.uk/2/hi/asia-pacific/6932801.stm)

370.

Emmy Rossum, Fiona in Shameless, sang frequently at the Metropolitan Opera when she was a kid, leading her to play Christine in the movie Phantom of the Opera.

Reference: (https://www.biography.com/people/emmy-rossum-21221637)

371.

One in five orthodontic patients needing braces is over age 18. The bones of adults have stopped growing, so some structural changes cannot be accomplished without surgery.

Reference: (https://www.health.harvard.edu/oral-health/are-you-too-old-for-braces)

372.

Shortly after finishing the filming of "Zombieland," Woody Harrelson had an altercation with a TMZ photographer. His defense was that he was still in character and thought that the cameraman was a zombie.

Reference: (https://en.wikipedia.org/wiki/Zombieland)

373.

Rude behavior by a doctor can cause an entire hospital team to make worse diagnoses and treatment decisions.

Reference: (http://time.com/4006317/rudeness-effect-hospital-patients/)

374.

Comedian Jackie Mason spent several years as a practicing Rabbi before becoming a comedian.

Reference: (http://people.com/archive/too-much-of-a-ham-to-remain-a-rabbi-broadways-jackie-mason-is-now-the-toast-of-the-town-vol-27-no-8/)

375.

The color red is the most popular color with flags around the world.

Reference: (http://time.com/patriotic-flag-colors/)

376.

Undocumented immigrants are required to register with Selective Service in the United States.

Reference: (https://www.sss.gov/Registration-Info/Who-Registration)

377.

The original Pac-Man game ran at just over 60 frames per second.

Reference: (https://en.wikipedia.org/wiki/Namco_Pac-Man)

378.

In 1657, Oliver Cromwel declined the offer of the office of Monarch of England, a position he helped abolish in the civil war, referring to the monarchy as a then-modern Jericho.

Reference:(https://wikipedia.org/wiki/List_of_people_who_have_declined_a_British_honour#Honours_declined)

379.

20th century women used their hat pins as weapons against men sexually harassing them.

Reference: (https://www.smithsonianmag.com/history/hatpin-peril-terrorized-men-who-couldnt-handle-20th-century-woman-180951219/)

380.

The "burpee" is named after the man who invented it as part of his PhD dissertation.

Reference: (https://en.wikipedia.org/wiki/Burpee_(exercise))

381.

When a domestic pig gets out into the wild, it will revert to a wild state in a matter of months, growing tusks, a hairy coat and becoming more aggressive.

Reference:(http://blog.mlive.com/flintjournal/outdoors/2007/11/domestic_pigs_quickly_revert_t.html)

382.

GIs in World War II accidentally spawned a religious cult among the Pacific Island natives.

Reference: (https://www.smithsonianmag.com/history/in-john-they-trust-109294882/)

383.

Potato chips cause more weight gain than any other food.

Reference: (https://caloriebee.com/nutrition/How-Healthy-is-McDonalds-The-Real-Story)

384.

Michael Jordan now makes more money each year than he earned in salary during his entire 15 year NBA career.

Reference: (http://www.businessinsider.com/michael-jordan-brand-nike-endorsements-2015-9)

385.

During World War II, more than a thousand Jewish refugees living in the Philippines avoided arrest and persecution by the Japanese forces because they were holding German passports and the Japanese couldn't perceive a difference between German nationals and German Jews.

Reference:(https://en.wikipedia.org/wiki/History_of_the_Jews_in_the_Philippines#Japanese_inv asion)

386.

The Dread Broadcasting Corporation is a pirate radio station started in west London in 1981. It is credited with being Britain's first black radio station.

Reference: (https://en.wikipedia.org/wiki/Dread_Broadcasting_Corporation)

387.

In "Back To The Future", the DeLorean's return trip was originally scripted to occur at a nuclear test site; and the bomb blast was to be the source for the needed 1.21 gigawatts, but they storyboarded the car driving into an atomic bomb blast.

Reference: (https://youtube.com/watch?v=Iqo7ytUzcao)

388.

There is no historical evidence that Betsy Ross had anything to do with making the first American Flag. In fact, the first mention of her having anything to do with making the first flag came almost 100 years later and was told by her grandson.

Reference: (https://www.history.org/Foundation/journal/Summer08/betsy.cfm)

389.

The main component of education in Turkmenistan has been almost completely replaced by memorization of the "Ruhnama," which is the president's personal autobiography. An engineer reported that all his son learns is passages.

Reference: (http://www.irinnews.org/feature/2003/07/09/focus-education)

390.

In Australia, Burger King is called Hungry Jack's.

Reference: (http://www.campaignbrief.com/2017/08/cb-exclusive-hungry-jacks-laun.html)

391.

California is the 6th largest economy in the world behind United States, China, Japan, Germany, and the United Kingdom. It's bigger than India, France, Brazil, Italy, Russia, Canada, Spain, Australia, South Korea, and Mexico.

392.

Jack Nicklaus earned $269,000 in his 6 wins at the Masters. This was less than last year's 10th place finisher. The winner earned $1.8 million dollars.

Reference: (http://mweb.cbssports.com/golf/eye-on-golf/25146033/masters-prize-money-set-at-10-million)

393.

A U.S. nuclear submarine that sank in deep water in 1968 is still resting at the bottom of the sea at a known location. Its nuclear reactor and nuclear weapons have never been recovered.

Reference: (https://en.wikipedia.org/wiki/USS_Scorpion_(SSN-589)?r=1#Environmental_concerns)

394.

Facial recognition is so advanced that CCTV pictures are compared to online pics and accurately identify us. Based on our face, opt-in marketing can give real-time coupons because we walked into a participating restaurant. Government has laws that protect us, but in the U.S., corporations have none.

Reference: (https://www.youtube.com/watch?v=mnfWZvU_Jqo)

395.

In 1981, horse meat labeled as beef was discovered at a plant that supplied hamburger and taco meat to Jack in the Box. The meat was originally from Australia, and during their checks on location, inspectors discovered other shipments destined for the U.S. that included kangaroo meat.

Reference: (https://en.wikipedia.org/wiki/Jack_in_the_Box#E._coli_outbreak)

396.

In 2007, in Singapore, oral and anal sex were legalized for heterosexuals and female homosexuals only.

Reference: (https://en.wikipedia.org/wiki/LGBT_rights_in_Singapore#Statutes)

397.

The Slovene alphabet doesn't have the letter "W."

Reference: (https://en.wikipedia.org/wiki/Slovene_alphabet)

398.

A Chinese doctor is seeking asylum in Germany after revealing that "more than 10,000" Chinese athletes were taking performance enhancing drugs in the 1980s and 1990s as part of a systemic doping scandal by the country.

Reference: (https://www.si.com/olympics/2017/10/24/chinese-doping-scandal-1980s-1990s-ard-broadcast)

399.

Earthworms have even been ranked the number one most influential species in the history of the planet, above dinosaurs and humans.

Reference: (https://theconversation.com/earthworms-are-more-important-than-pandas-if-you-want-to-save-the-planet-74010)

400.

In order to be fair to all religions, in addition to Bibles, kids in some Florida schools are also going to have access to literature from their local Satanic Temple.

Reference: (http://twentytwowords.com/heres-the-complete-satanic-activity-book-that-florida-school-children-are-being-given/)

401.

The surviving SEAL from the events that inspired Lone Survivor supports the Afghani man who saved him with royalties from the book.

Reference: (http://www.thedailybeast.com/articles/2013/11/08/the-afghan-village-that-saved-navy-seal-marcus-luttrell.html)

402.

The Golden Arches Theory of Conflict Prevention states that two countries containing at least one McDonald's are very unlikely to go to war with one another.

Reference: (http://www.nytimes.com/1996/12/08/opinion/foreign-affairs-big-mac-i.html)

403.

The fact that there are seven days to the week, internationally, and that the Sun day is followed by the Moon day, happened thanks to ancient Mesopotamia or Egypt passing it on to Greece, Rome, India, and Japan.

Reference: (http://www.cjvlang.com/Dow/dowjpn.html)

404.

Exposure to platinum can turn snails into their evolutionary decedents, the slug.

Reference: (http://www.wired.com/2010/10/snails-slugs-shell-evolution)

405.

Some heroin addicts, once free of their addiction, continue to inject water into their veins.

Reference: (https://www.vice.com/en_uk/read/heroin-addicts-who-cant-inject-heroin-238)

406.

Rwanda is testing a drone delivery service to deliver plasma and blood to hospitals. This will decrease the time it takes to deliver crucial supplies to remote areas.

Reference: (https://www.technologyreview.com/s/608034/blood-from-the-sky-ziplines-ambitious-medical-drone-delivery-in-africa/)

407.

Female praying mantises that cannibalizes the male during copulation produce more eggs than those who don't.

Reference: (https://gizmodo.com/why-female-praying-mantises-devour-their-partners-durin-1782818376)

408.

Between 1800 and 2009, tigers killed an estimated 373,000 humans.

Reference: (https://en.wikipedia.org/wiki/Tiger_attack)

409.

An African woman grew up in North Korea in exile. She speaks Korean as her first language and Kim Il Sung nagged her "like a typical grandfather." She ran away once from a white man when she realized that his accent was American.

Reference: (http://www.reuters.com/article/us-korea-north-macias-idUSBRE99108M20131002)

410.

The whistled language, Sylbo, is used to communicate long distances in the Canary Islands.

Reference: (https://www.youtube.com/watch?v=C0CIRCjoICA&t)

411.

Traffic on Winston Churchill Ave., near Gibraltar Airport, must stop to allow planes to cross the street as they are taking off and landing.

Reference: (https://wanderwisdom.com/transportation/Most-Dangerous-Airports)

412.

Spandau Ballet is the name given to the spasmodic "dance" that soldiers did in World War II after being shot by the German MG-42 machine gun.

Reference: (http://www.namepistol.com/bands/definitive-27-worst-band-names-ever-20-11.html)

413.

The potato chip was invented in 1853 by a Native American chef who was trying to rile a customer who had complained about his French fries being too thick.

Reference: (http://www.ideafinder.com/history/inventions/potatochips.htm)

414.

In Norway, to change your surname to one that 200 or fewer people have, you must ask from permission from everyone who has that name.

Reference: (http://www.skatteetaten.no/en/person/National-Registry/Change-of-name/Unrestricted-and-protected-surnames/)

415.

Most cats are lactose intolerant, despite cats being shown drinking milk in stories and TV shows.

Reference: (https://pets.webmd.com/cats/guide/cats-and-dairy-get-the-facts)

416.

Through 50 years of experimentation investigating the domestication of wolves, scientists in Russia successfully domesticated the Silver Fox; a breed of foxes that behave a lot like dogs.

Reference: (http://en.wikipedia.org/wiki/Domesticated_silver_fox)

417.

There is a man in New York City who mines sidewalk cracks for gold. He can make over $600 a week from doing this.

Reference: (http://nypost.com/2011/06/20/got-his-mined-in-the-gutter/)

418.

In 2003, a museum at Leigh on Sea mistook a Victorian drainage pipe for a 150,000-year-old 4foot long woolly mammoth tusk.

Reference: (http://www.megalithic.co.uk/article.php?sid=2146411092)

419.

In 1982, the University of Virginia's number 1 ranked men's basketball team suffered a regular season loss to Division 2 Chaminade University of Honolulu. It is widely considered the greatest upset in college basketball history.

Reference:(https://en.wikipedia.org/wiki/1982_Virginia_vs._Chaminade_men%27s_basketball_game)

420.

The Los Angeles Unified School District has an Arts and Artifacts Collection located in the LAPD headquarters. It holds millions of dollars' worth of art and other artifacts gifted to the school district.

Reference: (http://www.kcet.org/arts/artbound/counties/los-angeles/lausd-arts-archives-collection.html)

421.

There was a dinosaur with fingers like swords.

Reference: (http://en.wikipedia.org/wiki/Therizinosaurus#Description)

422.

A Norwegian 3rd division football team once traded one of their forwards to a rival team for his weight in shrimp.

Reference: (http://www.theintelligencer.com/news/article/Soccer-Player-Traded-for-Shrimp-10467296.php)

423.

If all the descendants of a pair of starfish survived and reproduced, then after just 16 years their population would exceed 10^{79}; which is the estimated number of electrons in the known universe.

Reference: (https://openlibrary.org/books/OL5798378M/Evolution)

424.

Before forming "The Doors," a 19 year old Jim Morrison acted in a promotional movie for Florida State University.

Reference: (https://www.thedoors.com/news/jim-morrison-appears-fsu-promo-video-1096)

425.

The youngest mother recorded giving birth was 5 year old, Lina Medina, in Peru. Her son, Gerardo, didn't discover that what he thought was his older sister was actually his mother, until the age of 10.

Reference: (https://en.wikipedia.org/wiki/Lina_Medina)

426.

The Flaming Lips released an EP on a literal human skull.

Reference: (https://www.discogs.com/The-Flaming-Lips-24-Hour-Song-Skull/release/3605303)

427.

During filming of The Wire, then-mayor Martin O'Malley called the show's creator, asked him to quit being so critical, and threatened to block filming in Baltimore.

Reference: (http://davidsimon.com/down-to-the-wire/)

428.

Chinese mathematician Yitang Shang couldn't get an academic job upon graduating, having to work as an accountant and a delivery worker for a New York City restaurant. He later went on to solve a math problem that had been unsolved for 150 years and won a MacArthur Genius Grant.

Reference: (https://en.wikipedia.org/wiki/Yitang_Zhang)

429.

Trademarking exists for more than twice as long as copyrighting. The first ever trademark dates back to the 13th century.

Reference: (https://en.wikipedia.org/wiki/Trademark)

430.

At least 1 in 4 people who say they've read George Orwell's 1984 are lying.

Reference: (https://www.youtube.com/watch?v=7y83UkvHpYk)

431.

In all tests of significance, the pie value needs to be less than 0.05 before it can be determined that there is a statistically significant relationship between two variables.

Reference: (https://cdn.southampton.ac.uk/assets/imported/transforms/content-block/UsefulDownloads_Download/C04DB441CDB34B209B1A14142FDAC245/PASSS%20RQ4%20Chi%20Square.pdf)

432.

A nightmare refers to a literal night mare. A "mare" is a demon which gives you bad dreams.

Reference: (http://en.wikipedia.org/wiki/Mare_%28folklore%29)

433.

In a housing experiment that moved families from poor neighborhood to wealthier ones, boys experienced PTSD rates comparable to those of combat soldiers, while psychological well-being improved for girls.

Reference: (http://www.newrepublic.com/article/116886/boys-report-ptsd-when-they-move-richer-neighborhoods)

434.

If you lose 75% of your liver, it'll grow back completely in one year.

Reference: (https://en.wikipedia.org/wiki/Liver_regeneration)

435.

The last name of "How to Win Friends and Influence People" author Dale Carnegie was not originally named Carnegie; in an example of how to influence people, he changed the spelling from Carnegey to resemble the name of the more influential Andrew Carnegie.

Reference: (https://en.wikipedia.org/wiki/Dale_Carnegie)

436.

Philosopher, Jeremy Bentham, requested that his body be preserved to be an "auto-icon" of himself. His remains are now seated in the University College London.

Reference: (https://www.ucl.ac.uk/Bentham-Project/who/autoicon)

437.

After learning of his parent's tragic death due to carbon monoxide poisoning, Weird Al went on to perform and gave the reason that, "since my music had helped many of my fans through tough times, maybe it would work for me as well".

Reference: (http://en.wikipedia.org/wiki/%22Weird_Al%22_Yankovic#Personal_life)

438.

There is a lake in South Carolina called "Alcohol and Drug Abuse Lake."

Reference: (https://geonames.usgs.gov/apex/f?p=gnispq:3:0::NO::P3_FID:1239107)

439.

In 2008 a man electrocuted his wife to death with nipple clamps. The death was ruled a homicide.

Reference: (http://www.wgal.com/article/coroner-sex-electrocution-death-homicide/6203305)

440.

A couple from the United Kingdom adopted 8 children from one family on their trip to Africa. They had 2 sons of their own before that.

Reference: (http://www.mirror.co.uk/news/uk-news/couple-set-world-adoption-record-3778436)

441.

Some antennas are designed using an algorithm that mimics Darwinian evolution.

Reference: (https://en.wikipedia.org/wiki/Evolved_antenna)

442.

The camel in the GEICO "Hump Day" ad, who's named Caleb, has been in multiple movies like Transformers 2 and has even been in a Macklemore and Ryan Lewis music video.

Reference: (https://www.cbsnews.com/8301-505270_162-57603417/hump-day-geico-commercial-creators-dish-on-ads-success-its-development/)

443.

In normal humans the overbite is about 3to 5 millimeters between the teeth. Overlaps greater than 5 millimeters are classified as an abnormal overbite. The overbites make up about 70 percent of the dental disorders in children making it the most common malocclusion.

Reference: (https://www.dental.net/dental-conditions/underbite-overbite-crossbite/)

444.

Here Comes the Mummies is a funk band that is rumored to have several Grammy winners among the members. They perform while wearing full mummy costumes so they can keep their identities "under wraps."

Reference: (https://en.wikipedia.org/wiki/Here_Come_the_Mummies)

445.

Emily Blunt developed a debilitating stutter in her childhood, which couldn't be cured by speech or relaxation coaches. It was cured when she was asked to speak in an accent in the school play.

Reference: (http://www.stutteringhelp.org/emily-blunt-talks-about-stuttering)

446.

Philadelphia is home to mass graves filled with bodies of 1918 flu victims.

Reference: (http://www.upenn.edu/gazette/1198/lynch3.html)

447.

The largest known volcano is on Mars and is the width of Arizona.

Reference: (https://amp.space.com/20133-olympus-mons-giant-mountain-of-mars.html)

448.

There is a sausage restaurant in Regensburg, Germany which is in business for 900 years. That means that they were selling sausages well before the Inca Empire existed and are still serving over 6,000 sausages a day.

Reference: (http://en.wikipedia.org/wiki/Regensburg_Sausage_Kitchen)

449.

Until 1990, homosexuals were banned from immigrating to the United States.

Reference: (http://cis.org/Immigration%2526Homosexuals-PolicyTowardHomosexuals)

450.

Richard Feynman, a physicist who worked on the Manhattan Project, was hounded by the FBI until he sent them a memo to leave him alone as he'd helped build the atomic bomb. When J. Edgar Hoover found out about it, he also sent out a memo telling them not to pursue Feynman unless told otherwise.

Reference: (https://www.atlasobscura.com/articles/when-a-physicist-asked-the-fbi-to-stop-calling-because-he-helped-make-the-atomic-bomb)

451.

The national anthem of Greece has 158 verses.

Reference: (https://thoughtcatalog.com/index.html)

452.

Roughly 26,500 pounds of human excrement is left on Mount Everest each season.

Reference: (https://www.washingtonpost.com/news/morning-mix/wp/2015/03/03/decades-of-human-waste-have-made-mount-everest-a-fecal-time-bomb/)

453.

A plasma contactor is used during all spacewalks from the ISS in order to protect the astronauts from electrical shock hazards.

Reference: (http://www.nasa.gov/centers/glenn/about/fs06grc.html)

454.

Elvis Presley's Graceland home is the second most-visited house in America with over 650,000 visitors a year; second only to the White House.

Reference: (https://en.wikipedia.org/wiki/Graceland)

455.

One of the first science fiction stories, "Description of a New World, Called a Blazing World," was written in 1666 by the Duchess Margaret Cavendish. She helped popularize scientific advancements, like the telescope and microscope, and was considered the first female philosopher of her time.

Reference: (https://www.atlasobscura.com/articles/one-of-the-earliest-science-fiction-books-was-written-in-the-1600s-by-a-duchess)

456.

In Canada, the term "Canadian Bacon" isn't used. The cut of meat from the loin is referred to as "back bacon." In Southern Ontario, "Peameal Bacon," is a similar product; however, it's not smoked but rather set in a brine.

Reference: (https://en.wikipedia.org/wiki/Back_bacon)

457.

There is a town in New York called Wales that is distinctly shaped exactly like the country that it's named after.

Reference: (https://en.wikipedia.org/wiki/Wales,_New_York)

458.

Robert Metcalfe, the inventor of Ethernet, predicted in 1995 that the Internet would suffer a "catastrophic collapse" the next year, promising to eat his words if it did not. In 1997, he blended a printed copy of his prediction with some liquid and drank it.

Reference: (https://en.wikipedia.org/wiki/Robert_Metcalfe#Incorrect_predictions)

459.

In future millennia, carbon dating specimens from our lifetime may not be possible because of the altering of current natural Carbon-14 levels by nuclear weapons and nuclear or fossil fuel power plants.

Reference:(http://www.acad.carleton.edu/curricular/BIOL/classes/bio302/pages/carbondatingback.html)

460.

If you follow the recommendations from the brewery, it takes over two minutes to pour a pint of Guinness.

Reference: (http://learn.kegerator.com/pouring-guinness/)

461.

Bone china actually contains animal bone.

Reference: (https://en.wikipedia.org/wiki/Bone_china)

462.

Robert De Niro tracked down and used Al Capone's tailor for The Untouchables.

Reference: (https://bamfstyle.com/2015/10/17/untouchables-capone-gray/)

463.

Cougars are the biggest cat that can purr and meow.

Reference: (https://youtu.be/BXhfZRE08ko)

464.

Tom Cruise vandalized the world's tallest building in 2010. During the filming of Mission Impossible 4, he climbed to the top of the Burj Khalifa without safety equipment and etched Katie Holmes' name into the spire.

Reference: (http://www.emirates247.com/entertainment/celebrity-gossip/did-cruise-etch-graffiti-on-the-tip-of-burj-khalifa-2011-12-15-1.432913)

465.

The O.J. Simpson car chase led to, at the time, the busiest day in Domino's Pizza.

Reference: (http://www.businessinsider.com/how-oj-simpson-boosted-dominos-sales-2014-6)

466.

During World War II, a U.S. ship containing 120,000 pounds of mustard gas was destroyed, leaking the contents off the coast of Italy. Research of the effects of this tragedy led to the development of Chemo drugs.

Reference: (http://fly.historicwings.com/2012/12/deadly-mystery-at-bari/)

467.

The total mass of the asteroid belt is approximately 4% that of the Moon.

Reference: (https://en.wikipedia.org/wiki/Asteroid_belt)

468.

Prior to 2004, if a United States citizen was working in Mexico for a U.S. based company, they were forced to pay into both the U.S. and Mexican Social Security system. The rule applied to Mexicans working for Mexican based companies inside the U.S. as well.

Reference: (https://www.ssa.gov/pressoffice/pr/USandMexico-pr.htm)

469.

Children with gray hair might have a B-12 deficiency.

Reference: (http://www.drgreene.com/qa-articles/children-gray-hair/)

470.

Several surveys find that more marriages ended over financial tensions than other reasons. Sex and love play less role in relationships.

Reference: (https://www.cnbc.com/2017/01/31/so-its-money--not-sex--that-can-bust-up-your-relationship.html)

471.

Up to 1 billion birds are killed per year in collisions with buildings. This is the second greatest human-caused source of bird deaths, with pet and feral cats killing more.

Reference: (https://abcbirds.org/article/up-to-one-billion-birds-may-be-killed-annually-in-building-collisions-new-study-says/)

472.

There are marine ecological "Dead Zones" that correspond globally to intensive economic use areas.

Reference: (https://en.wikipedia.org/wiki/Dead_zone_(ecology))

473.

The largest existing snail is the "Syrinx Aruanus" and it weighs up to 39 pounds.

Reference: (https://en.wikipedia.org/wiki/Syrinx_aruanus)

474.

Mr. Brightside by The Killers never left the U.K. charts. In fact, it was among the top 50 even in 2017.

Reference: (https://noisey.vice.com/en_us/article/pg78ky/the-killers-mr-brightside-not-left-uk-charts-since-2004)

475.

Miami is the only major U.S. city founded by a woman.

Reference: (https://www.huffingtonpost.com/2013/05/12/julia-tuttle-miami-mother-of-miami_n_3262488.html)

476.

Ferdinand Demara, an imposter, served on a Canadian warship under a false identity. When a group of injured soldiers needed surgery, he successfully pulled it off by reading the medical handbook a few days before.

Reference:(http://content.time.com/time/specials/packages/article/0,28804,1900621_1900618_1900605,00.html)

477.

The graphite bomb is a non-lethal weapon that can be delivered through a warhead, causing failure in electrical power systems by spreading a cloud of fine carbon particles that encourage arcing and short-circuiting between power lines.

Reference: (https://en.wikipedia.org/wiki/Graphite_bomb)

478.

Psychologists recognize "the need for drama" as a personality trait. High NFD individuals agree with statements like, "Sometimes it's fun to get people riled up".

Reference: (https://www.theguardian.com/lifeandstyle/2016/jul/29/oliver-burkeman-need-for-drama-barack-obama)

479.

Steve Vai, who played the devil's ace in "Crossroads" turned 6 years old on 6/6/66.

Reference: (https://www.youtube.com/watch?v=cfXZeOHp5So&feature=youtu.be&t=2m2s)

480.

The emperor penguin can dive to a depth of 1,850 feet. That's deeper than any other bird and deeper than the operational range of most naval submarines.

Reference: (http://animals.nationalgeographic.com/animals/birds/emperor-penguin/)

481.

Nearly 30% of Americans believe an armed rebellion might be necessary in order to protect liberties.

Reference: (http://rt.com/usa/americans-revolution-armed-percent-738/)

482.

In the United States Postal Service Remote Encoding Facility, workers try to determine the destination of mail with poorly written addresses.

Reference:(http://www.slate.com/blogs/atlas_obscura/2015/05/19/unreadable_mail_ends_up_at_the_usps_remote_encoding_facility_in_salt_lake.html)

483.

The McCullough effect is a visual phenomenon which, if induced for 15 minutes, can alter your color perception to adapt to colors not actually present for over 3 months.

Reference: (https://en.wikipedia.org/wiki/McCollough_effect)

484.

The ideal cut diamond is made to reflect the light back towards the crown. The angle is between 39.7 to 41.7 degrees.

Reference: (http://www.uniteddiamonds.com/info_pages/diamond_education/index-learn-diamonds-cut.html)

485.

The landscape photographer, Peter Lik, has sold his picture "Phantom" for $6.5 million dollars, setting a new record for the most expensive photograph of all time.

Reference: (http://www.theguardian.com/artanddesign/jonathanjonesblog/2014/dec/10/most-expensive-photograph-ever-hackneyed-tasteless)

486.

There is an actual university where you can study science fiction and fantasy literature with a concentration in Tolkien Studies.

Reference: (https://signumuniversity.org/departments/language-literature/tolkien-studies/)

487.

Tylenol doesn't relieve inflammation.

Reference: (https://medlineplus.gov/ency/article/002123.htm)

488.

There is an award in Australia presented to the perpetrator of the most preposterous piece of paranormal or pseudoscientific piffle, called the Bent Spoon Award.

Reference: (https://en.wikipedia.org/wiki/Bent_Spoon_Award)

489.

In 2014, Intel worked with Stephen Hawking to upgrade the program that he uses to talk to the world, but he refused to change the speech synthesizer board that gives him his iconic voice.

Reference: (http://www.wired.com/2015/01/intel-gave-stephen-hawking-voice/)

490.

Contrary to popular belief, the British have healthier teeth compared to Americans.

Reference: (https://melmagazine.com/my-bad-british-teeth-are-healthier-than-yours-so-there-a395df527184)

491.

Marjory Stoneman Douglas fought against efforts to drain the Florida Everglades and reclaim land for development when she was 79 years old. Her tireless efforts earned her several variations of the nickname "Grande Dame of the Everglades." She also received the Presidential Medal of Freedom.

Reference: (https://en.wikipedia.org/wiki/Marjory_Stoneman_Douglas)

492.

The open end of a noose is called a "Honda."

Reference: (https://en.wikipedia.org/wiki/Noose)

493.

Peter the Great issued a decree that every monastery was required to produce vodka, infused with horseradish, and provide it to its employees, particularly those who performed hard labor and worked in the cold weather.

Reference: (http://www.hrenom.ru/)

494.

Panthers are not a species. Panther is just the name given to any melanistic big cat, for example, black jaguars are sometimes called panthers.

Reference: (https://nerdist.com/black-panthers-are-not-a-species-so-what-are-they/)

495.

There was a failed Wild West outlaw nicknamed "Little Dick".

Reference: (https://en.wikipedia.org/wiki/Richard_West_(outlaw))

496.

The highest observable temperature in the universe was briefly seen at the Large Hadron Collider at CERN. Its magnitude was 7.2 trillion degrees Fahrenheit.

Reference: (http://www.fromquarkstoquasars.com/what-is-the-highest-known-temperature/)

497.

A Roman merchant who sold fake jewels was sentenced to face a lion in the arena. When the gate finally opened, a chicken walked out. Emperor Gallienus proclaimed, "He practiced deceit and then had it practiced on him."

Reference: (http://www.smithsonianmag.com/history/secrets-of-the-colosseum-75827047/)

498.

The world's poorest man is Jerome Kerviel, who owes French bank Societe Generale $6.3 billion for fraudulent trades.

Reference: (https://www.theatlantic.com/business/archive/2012/11/meet-the-most-indebted-man-in-the-world/264413/)

499.

Although the U.S. only produces about 2% of the world's rice, it is one of the biggest exporters of rice.

Reference: (https://www.youtube.com/watch?v=yfM75D0cikg)

500.

Margarine was illegal in Wisconsin until 1967.

Reference: (http://host.madison.com/wsj/news/local/govt-and-politics/wisconsin-ban-on-margarine-targeted-for-repeal/article_e7cc94be-e2e7-11e0-ac81-001cc4c002e0.html)

501.

In 2003, a German citizen, whose name is similar to that of a terrorist, was captured by the CIA while traveling on a vacation, then tortured and raped in detention.

Reference:(http://cmiskp.echr.coe.int/tkp197/view.asp?action=html&documentId=875676&portal=hbkm&source=externalbydocnumber&table=F69A27FD8FB86142BF01C1166DEA398649)

502.

Actor Keanu Reeves was forced into doing the film "The Watcher" when his assistant Brian forged his signature on a contract. He performed the role rather than get involved in a lengthy legal battle.

Reference: (https://en.wikipedia.org/wiki/The_Watcher_%28film%29)

503.

On September 25th, 2000, NBA player Paul Pierce was stabbed 11 times in the face, neck, and back and had a bottle smashed over his head. On November 1st, Pierce played the season opener scoring 28 points and went on to play in every game that season.

Reference: (https://en.wikipedia.org/wiki/Paul_Pierce#Stabbing_incident)

504.

Frilled sharks have 25 rows that maintain 300 triangular shaped needle sharp teeth. One such shark that was recently dissected revealed a diet of squid, cuttlefish, octopus and other sharks. It's believed that their diet is more than 60% cephalopods.

Reference: (http://www.sharksider.com/frilled-shark/)

505.

The Indian state of Goa was ruled by Portugal for hundreds of years, seceding to India in the 1970s. As a result, a large number of people there still speak Portuguese, and are entitled to dual Portuguese citizenship.

Reference: (https://en.wikipedia.org/wiki/Goa)

506.

The English surname Featherstonhaugh is pronounced "Fanshaw".

Reference: (https://en.wikipedia.org/wiki/Featherstonhaugh)

507.

Thunderstorms can produce glowing orbs called "ball lightning." Though still largely unexplained, these "luminous spheres" move around for a few seconds and then disappear.

Reference: (https://www.britannica.com/science/ball-lightning)

508.

Lojban is a constructed language based on formal logic and was designed to be neutral between cultures allowing you to communicate more concisely, such as being gender neutral, no tenses, and the ability to speak in emoticons.

Reference: (https://en.wikipedia.org/wiki/Lojban)

509.

There is an animal called an Okapi, which has the body of a horse, the stripes of a zebra on its body and the head of a giraffe.

Reference: (http://www.factzoo.com/mammals/okapi-part-zebra-giraffe-horse-herbivore.html)

510.

On three occasions, the Earth was completely covered with ice. Scientists refer to it as "Snowball Earth."

Reference: (https://news.cnrs.fr/articles/when-earth-was-a-snowball)

511.

Japanese Tempura has its origins in Portugal.

Reference: (https://en.wikipedia.org/wiki/Tempura#Origins)

512.

Norway had to close a tunnel because it was full of burning cheese.

Reference: (http://www.bbc.com/news/world-europe-21141244)

513.

Coca-Cola was originally marketed for whites, while Pepsi was marketed for blacks.

514.

21-year-old Lieutenant Zvika Greengold, an Israeli tank officer who fought in the Yom Kippur War for 30 hours straight, destroyed up to 60 enemy tanks, swapping his own every time he sustained damage. He fooled the Syrians into believing they were facing a company sized force.

Reference: (http://www.jpost.com/Arab-Israeli-Conflict/I-was-willing-to-die-to-stop-the-Syrian-advance-416734)

515.

Canada has a post called Administrator of Canada. If the Governor General dies, is incapacitated, or out of the country, the Chief Justice of the Supreme Court of Canada can be appointed Administrator and fulfill the duties of the Governor General until a new one is appointed.

Reference: (https://en.wikipedia.org/wiki/Deputy_of_the_Governor_General_of_Canada)

516.

Jousting is Maryland's official state sport.

Reference: (http://marylandjousting.com/)

517.

A man died while cleaning machinery with gasoline, which dripped onto a rat that was running across the floor. The rat's gasoline-covered fur ignited when it ran beneath a heart with a pilot light, causing an explosion that killed the worker. This is a story of negligence that is now taught in law school.

Reference: (http://abnormaluse.com/2012/06/the-flaming-rat-case-a-revisonist-analysis.html)

518.

There are internet domains for the Soviet Union, East-Germany and Yugoslavia. Those domains were created a few months before the communist bloc collapsed.

Reference: (https://www.inverse.com/article/8672-the-bizarre-afterlife-of-su-the-domain-name-and-last-bastion-of-the-ussr)

519.

Cascadia is a proposed independent state in the Pacific Northwest focused on ecological sustainability that's supported by a number of organizations.

Reference: (https://www.cascadianow.org/)

520.

John Holahan, the creator of the Lucky Charms cereal, came up with the idea after a visit to the grocery store in which he decided to mix Cheerios with bits of Brach's Circus Peanuts.

Reference: (https://en.wikipedia.org/wiki/Lucky_Charms#History)

521.

An accountant murdered his client, a $5 million dollar lottery winner, because he was pushed over the edge by her continued wasteful spending.

Reference: (http://www.heraldsun.com.au/news/national/lotto-winner-killed-over-wasteful-habits/story-fndo317g-1226474386865)

522.

During the liberation war of Bangladesh in 1971, Pakistani soldiers killed 3 million Bangladeshi in one of the worst genocides in history. The United States took Pakistan's side, which they regretted later.

Reference: (http://www.southasiaanalysis.org/node/1431)

523.

Abraham Lincoln was the tallest U.S. President at 6'4", while James Madison was the shortest at 5'4".

Reference: (http://www.presidenstory.com/stat_tal.php)

524.

There is a Svalbard Global Seed Vault in Norway where the seeds of the world are kept in case of a global catastrophe.

Reference: (https://en.wikipedia.org/wiki/Svalbard_Global_Seed_Vault)

525.

In 2013, former Google China Chief Kai-fu-Lee posted an April Fool's prank that said people in China can get onto Facebook and Twitter, since both were long blocked by Internet censorship. When users clicked on the image, the text read, "I'm in Taipei, I'm in Taipei, I'm in Taipei, Happy April Fool's Day!"

Reference: (http://blogs.wsj.com/chinarealtime/2013/04/01/twitter-facebook-accessible-in-china-check-the-date/)

526.

In 1983, an F-15 fighter aircraft successfully landed with only one wing intact, after the other had been ripped off in a mid-air collision during a training flight.

Reference: (https://youtube.com/watch?v=M359poNjvVA)

527.

The Dunning-Kruger Effect was initially based on a bank robber who thought lemon juice would make his face invisible to security cameras.

Reference: (https://en.wikipedia.org/wiki/Dunning%E2%80%93Kruger_effect#Original_study)

528.

There is a site that offers a fake internet girlfriend service for $250 a month. This includes setting up a profile on a social networking site like Facebook to publicly communicate with you, making up to 2 public phone calls and getting about 10 text messages.

Reference: (http://www.fakeinternetgirlfriend.com/)

529.

The Crips street gang was originally formed as a Neighborhood Watch to eliminate criminal gangs by force.

Reference: (https://themortempost.wordpress.com/2014/01/07/the-crips-street-gang-was-originally-created-in-order-to-form-a-neighbourhood-watch-and-clear-the-streets-of-marauding-gangs/)

530.

Hyenas get fear based erections.

Reference: (https://youtu.be/wLE71i4JJiM?t=1h38m44s)

531.

Compton had only one black resident in 1930.

Reference: (https://en.wikipedia.org/wiki/Compton,_California#History)

532.

You can ski or snowboard in Hawaii.

Reference: (http://www.hawaiisnowskiclub.com/Mk/)

533.

There was Russian novel published in 1999 which re-tells The Lord of The Rings from Sauron's Perspective.

Reference: (http://en.wikipedia.org/wiki/The_Last_Ringbearer)

534.

Less than 1% of natural uranium is suitable for nuclear applications.

Reference: (https://www.youtube.com/watch?v=VIL5qi2ZRP0&feature=youtu.be)

535.

Indigenous Native Americans were not granted U.S. citizenship until 1924.

Reference: (https://constitutioncenter.org/blog/on-this-day-in-1924-all-indians-made-united-states-citizens)

536.

The term "posse" is actually a technical term in law. It comes from the Latin "posse comitatus" which means, "power of authority in the country."

Reference: (http://www.merriam-webster.com/dictionary/posse)

537.

It's illegal to pump your own gas in Oregon and New Jersey.

Reference: (http://www.phillyvoice.com/why-pumping-gas-illegal-new-jersey/)

538.

Adolescent rats drink more alcohol with their peers than adult rats with theirs.

Reference: (http://www.bbc.co.uk/programmes/b09pl662)

539.

A bald eagle somehow made its way to Ireland in 1987 and was so tired that it had to be returned via airplane.

Reference: (http://articles.latimes.com/1987-12-22/news/mn-30780_1_bald-eagle)

540.

In 1968, the Democratic National Convention selected Hubert Humphrey as the party's nominee, even though he hadn't entered a single primary.

541.

Actor Don Johnson was caught in Germany with $8 billion dollars in securities and credit notes.

Reference: (http://articles.latimes.com/2003/mar/13/local/me-johnson13)

542.

The North Korean show "It's So Funny" is one of the world's longest-running television comedies. It has been on air since the 1970s.

Reference: (https://en.wikipedia.org/wiki/It%27s_So_Funny)

543.

In 1997, Kleberg County, Texas voted unanimously to adopt "Heaven-O" as the county's official greeting. The resolution was the result of years of campaigning by local resident Leonso Canales who opposed the use of "Hello" because it contained the word "Hell."

Reference: (http://www.nytimes.com/1997/01/26/nyregion/hell-o-catching-up-with-a-ban-on-cursing.html)

544.

A tick bite can cause a lifetime allergy to red meat. The Lone Star tick injects a type of sugar found in red meat into the blood, and causes antibodies to be made that cause an allergic reaction when the person later ingests meat with the sugar.

Reference: (http://www.newyorker.com/tech/elements/can-ticks-make-you-allergic-to-red-meat)

545.

Some Hiroshima survivors grew "black fingernails", which were strange rod-shaped fingernails that contained active blood vessels and bled profusely when they broke off.

Reference: (http://www.pcf.city.hiroshima.jp/outline/index.php?l=E&id=34)

546.

The Philippines Sea Plate is converging with the continent at 7 centimeters or 2.75 inches per year in the west North West direction.

Reference: (https://en.wikipedia.org/wiki/Geology_of_Taiwan)

547.

The actor who played Scarlett O'Hara's love interest Ashley Wilkes in "Gone with the Wind" was less than a year younger than the actor who played Scarlett's father.

Reference: (https://en.wikipedia.org/wiki/Thomas_Mitchell_(actor))

548.

After position, velocity, and acceleration, the fourth derivative of position is called "jerk" and is measured with a "jerk meter."

Reference: (https://en.wikipedia.org/wiki/Jerk_(physics)#Jerk_in_manufacturing)

549.

In 1967, a 26 year old Australian Nurse used borrowed money to buy a plane which she flew into the Outback to eradicate Polio. She died at age 35 of cancer, and is remembered as one of the Great Women Pilots of the 20th century

Reference: (http://en.wikipedia.org/wiki/Robin_Miller_%28nurse%29#Biography)

550.

The Sun, when recordings are sped up, has a deep roaring sound.

Reference: (https://www.youtube.com/watch?v=CcuZD0A7RwM&feature=youtu.be)

551.

An ex-Judge was on trial on charges that he used a penis pump on himself in the courtroom while sitting in judgment of others.

Reference: (http://www.nbcnews.com/id/13599320/ns/us_news-crime_and_courts/t/ex-judges-trial-brings-lurid-charges-court/)

552.

The earliest known usage of the word "bullshit" was in the tittle of an unpublished T.S. Elliot poem.

Reference: (https://en.wikipedia.org/wiki/Bullshit#Etymology)

553.

One of the first sexologists suffered from impotence, until he discovered that he could easily be aroused by urinating on a woman.

Reference: (https://en.wikipedia.org/wiki/Havelock_Ellis#Marriage)

554.

In 2015, France passed a law to address planned obsolescence which requires companies to replace any defective products within 2 years, free of charge. This was the first time any legislature in the world openly acknowledged the existence of planned obsolescence.

Reference: (https://en.wikipedia.org/wiki/Planned_obsolescence#Future)

555.

American Express once granted Wayne Boden a credit card. He is a convicted serial killer from Canada known as "The Vampire Rapist" that's currently serving a life sentence.

Reference: (https://en.wikipedia.org/wiki/Wayne_Boden#Conviction,_imprisonment,_and_death)

556.

There are no women players in the Top 100 Go players.

Reference: (http://www.axialflow.com/projects.htm)

557.

Taco Bell released a statement on April 1st, 1996, claiming that they had bought the Liberty Bell and were renaming it the "Taco Liberty Bell." It was later revealed to be an April Fool's prank.

Reference: (http://www.ushistory.org/libertybell/bellhoax.html)

558.

Macadamia nuts are also known as bush nuts in Australia.

Reference: (http://www.bauplemuseum.com/bopple%20nut%20pub.pdf)

559.

Adam Young, who is also known as Owl City, was living in his parents' basement when he created the song "Fireflies".

Reference: (http://www.nytimes.com/2009/11/21/arts/music/21owl.html)

560.

Dennis Wilson, the only member of the Beach Boys who could actually surf, died by drowning.

Reference: (http://en.wikipedia.org/wiki/Dennis_Wilson#Charles_Manson)

561.

Every year, Finland increases in surface area by about 7 square kilometers because it is rebounding from the weight of ice age glaciers and rising out of the sea.

Reference: (http://en.wikipedia.org/w/index.php?title=Finland#Geography)

562.

The United States Air Force strapped a GoPro in the bomb bay of a B-52 and recorded the impact.

Reference: (https://www.youtube.com/watch?v=V0FPqdsC8_Y)

563.

The Chinese Government "encouraged" the country's tallest female basketball player to marry the country's tallest man. Their child was Yao Ming.

Reference: (http://www.smh.com.au/news/basketball/yao-ming-the-basketball-giant-made-in-china-by-order-of-the-state/2006/01/18/1137553645228.html)

564.

A Canadian college installed sleep pods for students to nap in the library. The units are not sound-proof at all and have been placed directly next to computer workstations, which the school hopes will help prevent any bad behavior.

Reference: (http://www.cbc.ca/news/canada/british-columbia/bcit-sleep-pods-library-1.3704552)

565.

The FedEx logo has won over 40 design awards and was ranked as one of the eight best logos in the last 35 years. The white arrow in the logo was an intentional design choice, created by blending two different fonts together.

Reference: (https://www.fastcodesign.com/1671067/the-story-behind-the-famous-fedex-logo-and-why-it-works)

566.

Albert Camus's accidental death might have been an elaborate KGB assassination.

Reference: (http://www.theguardian.com/books/2011/aug/07/albert-camus-killed-by-kgb)

567.

Modern container ships are slower than 19th century clippers.

Reference: (http://www.theguardian.com/environment/2010/jul/25/slow-ships-cut-greenhouse-emissions)

568.

Drinking is good for men. Men drinking even as much as a bottle of wine per day will live longer and healthier than people who don't drink at all. However, this is completely opposite for women.

Reference: (https://www.substance.com/truth-we-wont-admit-drinking-is-healthy/10285/)

569.

The Korean word "Han" is described as an all-encompassing sense of bitterness, a mixture of angst, endurance and a yearning for revenge that tests a person's soul.

Reference: (http://articles.latimes.com/2011/jan/05/world/la-fg-south-korea-han-20110105)

570.

The abbreviation "OMG" was first used in a 1917 letter to Winston Churchill.

Reference: (http://www.goratings.org/)

571.

Falconers will allow male falcons to copulate with their head when they need to breed from an imprinted bird.

Reference: (https://en.wikipedia.org/wiki/Imprinting_(psychology)#Sexual_imprinting)

572.

An Idahoan student made a science project about the dangers of dihydrogen monoxide, which is water. The project was so convincing that it caused his fellow students to call for it to be banned. This was used as an argument against leading the public to false conclusions with the manipulation of facts.

Reference: (http://mentalfloss.com/article/501907/14-year-old-who-convinced-people-ban%C2%A0dihydrogen-monoxide)

573.

Honey badgers' skins are so tough that spears and arrows are almost useless against them, and it's commonly held that the only certain way to kill them is, "a direct shot in the head with a fairly powerful rifle."

Reference: (https://www.biodiversitylibrary.org/item/35416#page/134/mode/1up)

574.

During prohibition, a jury that had heard a bootlegging case was itself put on trial after it drank the evidence. They said they did it to determine whether or not it contained alcohol.

Reference: (http://en.wikipedia.org/wiki/10_Things_You_Don%27t_Know_About)

575.

In 1998, a man was tricked into being in a Japanese reality show where he was kept solitary in a room for 15 months until he could win a $10,000 sweepstakes prize. Also, he had to be naked the entire time and he had no idea that he was being broadcast on TV, which means that he was watched by millions of people.

Reference: (http://en.wikipedia.org/wiki/Nasubi)

576.

Orcas, formerly known as killer whales, are actually dolphins, and they are the largest of the dolphin family.

Reference: (https://en.wikipedia.org/wiki/Killer_whale)

577.

The first atomic explosion in the United States was delayed by over two hours because the switchboard operator who was supposed to be controlling all the phone calls in Alamogordo, New Mexico was asleep on a sofa.

Reference: (https://alexandria-library.space/files/Ebooks/ComputerScience/Hacking/The%20Best%20of%202600%20-%20A%20Hacker%20Odyssey.pdf)

578.

The Weber Grill has its iconic shape because it was made from parts normally used to make buoys in the inventor's metal shop.

Reference: (https://en.wikipedia.org/wiki/Weber-Stephen_Products?buoy)

579.

According to Article VIII of the Outer Space Treaty of 1967, you can be charged for a crime committed anywhere in the known universe.

Reference: (http://www.businessinsider.com/heres-what-happens-if-you-commit-a-crime-in-outer-space-2014-1)

580.

The last words of Oklahoma City bomber Timothy McVeigh were, "I am the master of my fate, I am the captain of my soul." They were spoken as his last statement the day of his execution.

Reference: (https://www.theguardian.com/world/2001/jun/11/mcveigh.usa1)

581.

Surgeons in The Republic of Georgia replaced a cancer patient's amputated penis with a "fully-functioning" substitute made from skin grafts and the man's middle finger. He has two girlfriends and a full sex life.

Reference: (https://www.news24.com/xArchive/Archive/Finger-replacement-for-penis-20010215)

582.

The town of Elkader in Iowa is named after Abdelkader El Djezairi, a Sufi leader who formed an insurgent campaign against the French in Algeria. Abdelkader also received a golden shotgun from the United Kingdom and 2 engraved pistols from Lincoln.

Reference: (https://en.wikipedia.org/wiki/Abdelkader_El_Djezairi#Image_and_legacy)

583.

The critically endangered Hawksbill sea turtle is the only kind of its species that feed on sea sponges. They are crucial in maintaining the health of the ecosystems on and off land.

Reference: (http://www.seeturtles.org/hawksbill-turtles/)

584.

There is a Frisbee golf course in Antarctica.

Reference: (https://www.dgcoursereview.com/course.php?id=2120)

585.

The Royal Navy used a recruitment tactic known as Impressment, where press gangs would give the kings shilling to unsuspecting men. Possession of the coin was considered acceptance of your enlistment. The gangs often used devious methods such as dropping it into drinks and forcing it into drunk's hands.

Reference: (http://www.welcometoportsmouth.co.uk/press%20gangs.html)

586.

There are now about $1.2 billion dollar coin assets in the Federal Reserve vaults.

Reference: (http://www.npr.org/2011/06/28/137394348/-1-billion-that-nobody-wants)

587.

There is an oil field in Northern Iraq that has been burning for 2,500 years.

Reference: (https://en.wikipedia.org/wiki/Baba_Gurgur#Eternal_Fire)

588.

Leif Erikson Day is an actual day, it is observed October 9th. It honors Leif Erikson the Norse explorer who led the first Europeans thought to have set foot in continental North America.

Reference: (https://en.wikipedia.org/wiki/Leif_Erikson_Day)

589.

The first man to go over the Niagara Falls in a barrel died after slipping on an orange peel.

Reference: (https://adventure.howstuffworks.com/survival/wilderness/niagara6.htm)

590.

Stephen King wrote "Carrie" on an old typewriter while living in a trailer. He threw away the first 3 pages thinking he had written "the world's all time loser." His wife fished the pages out and pushed him to finish it. It turned out to be his first published novel.

Reference: (http://en.wikipedia.org/wiki/Carrie_%28novel%29)

591.

Newgrange in Ireland is older than both Stonehenge and the pyramids in Giza. On the morning of the winter solstice every year, the rising Sun shines down the entrance passageway and illuminates the burial chamber at the end. This only happens for a few minutes, once a year.

Reference: (http://en.wikipedia.org/w/index.php?title=Newgrange)

592.

There is a formal word "kayfabe" for portrayal of staged events and relationships in wrestling and has been very rarely broken. Kayfabe was a fiercely guarded secret for decades even outside the stage, but is more relaxed in a post-internet era.

Reference: (https://en.wikipedia.org/wiki/Kayfabe)

593.

The song "Bad Things" by Camila Cabello and MGK takes its chorus from a Fastball song from the 1990s called "Out of My Head".

Reference: (https://www.billboard.com/articles/columns/rock/7542085/fastball-out-of-my-head-interview-mgk-camila-cabello-bad-things-sample)

594.

The Arizona House of Representative's requires in their official rules that a prayer be read before every session.

Reference: (http://www.azleg.state.az.us/hrules.htm)

595.

The Queen of England's portrait has been on enough international banknotes to make a progressive timeline of her aging.

Reference: (http://mentalfloss.com/article/52759/15-international-banknotes-show-queen-elizabeth%E2%80%99s-aging-process)

596.

Chinese drinkers consume about three standard drinks on average per day, which is more than the Brits, Americans, Germans or Australians.

Reference: (http://www.scmp.com/lifestyle/health/article/1742243/changes-chinas-alcohol-use-policies-urgently-needed-researchers-say)

597.

Each time you recall a memory, it changes slightly.

Reference: (https://www.youtube.com/watch?v=qyb8Ah3jChw)

598.

The oldest Baby Boomers in the United States are now 70 years old.

Reference: (http://www.cdc.gov/nchs/fastats/life-expectancy.htm)

599.

In 1992, an Australian consortium tried to corner a $24 million Virginia Lotto and bought 2.4 million of the 7 million combinations.

Reference: (http://money.cnn.com/2016/01/11/news/powerball-jackpot-win-guarantee/index.html)

600.

Former U.S. President Theodore Roosevelt decided to move to Dakota to become a "cowboy" after his mother and wife died not even 12 hours apart, making him want to live a different life entirely. Roosevelt even had his own "cowboy suit" specifically made for him before he left on his journey.

Reference: (http://cowboytocowboy.com/wordpress/2016/09/30/the-cowboy-president/)

601.

The U.S. is not part of the International Criminal Court, which punishes war criminals and the "perpetrators of the worst crimes known to humankind".

Reference: (https://en.wikipedia.org/wiki/United_States_and_the_International_Criminal_Court)

602.

Melanie Griffith lived with a lion, was attacked by a lioness and required 50 facial stitches.

Reference: (http://mashable.com/2014/10/06/yes-thats-just-the-pet-lion-in-the-swimming-pool/?utm_cid=mash-com-fb-main-link#p8ZKK_yUakq3)

603.

The police chief of Crisfield, Maryland, burned down two city blocks and was caught taking bribes from drug dealers in 1987. However, he was released from prison after a week to fight the Gulf War.

Reference: (http://articles.baltimoresun.com/1990-11-16/news/1990320156_1_crisfield-swift-somerset-county)

604.

Indian housewives hold 11% of the world's gold. That is more than the reserves of the U.S., IMF, Switzerland and Germany put together.

Reference: (https://instanerd.me/v/77/indian-housewives-hold-11-of-the-world-s-gold)

605.

The scientist John von Neumann could, by the age of 6, divide two 8 digit numbers in his head and converse in ancient Greek. He published over 150 papers during his lifetime, and is considered by many to be among the most intelligent humans to have ever lived.

Reference: (https://en.wikipedia.org/wiki/John_von_Neumann)

606.

California's official state animal is extinct.

Reference: (http://en.wikipedia.org/wiki/California_grizzly_bear)

607.

In 2007, a Bowhead whale was discovered with the head of an explosive harpoon embedded deep under its neck blubber. The projectile was manufactured in New Bedford, Massachusetts in 1890.

Reference: (http://www.loe.org/shows/segments.html?programID=07-P13-00024&segmentID=7)

608.

The voice of phone numbers, voicemail, etc. is not a computer but the recorded voice of an actual lady named Joan Kenley.

Reference: (http://www.king5.com/mobile/article/entertainment/television/programs/evening/throwback-to-1996-joan-kenley-the-voice-of-voice-mail/281-188269346)

609.

CBS bought the New York Yankees in 1964. However, the Yankees struggled, so they sold it in 1973 to George Steinbrenner, who owned the team until his death in 2010.

Reference: (https://en.wikipedia.org/wiki/List_of_New_York_Yankees_owners_and_executives)

610.

Michigan has had an anti sodomy law in the legislature since 1931.

Reference: (http://legislature.mi.gov/doc.aspx?mcl-750-158)

611.

The network of neurons of the gut is as extensive and complex as the one in the spinal cord.

Reference: (http://www.scientificamerican.com/article/gut-feelings-the-second-brain-in-our-gastrointestinal-systems-excerpt/)

612.

Like hearing and eyesight, our sense of touch weakens when we get older. Some doctors believe that we lose around one percent of our tactile sense every year.

Reference: (http://www.huffingtonpost.com.au/entry/neuroscience-touch_n_6489050)

613.

The peanut butter and jelly sandwich was invented in 1901 by Julia Davis Chandler.

Reference: (http://nationalpeanutboard.org/news/who-invented-the-peanut-butter-and-jelly-sandwich.htm)

614.

Cuba's infant mortality rate is among the lowest in the world. In 2015, Cuba's infant mortality rate was 4.3 per 1,000 live births, with 535 child deaths out of 125,064 births recorded in the year.

Reference: (http://ahtribune.com/world/americas/321-cuba-infant-mortality-rate.html)

615.

Christian Atheists believe in the teachings of Christ but not that they were divinely inspired. They see Jesus as a humanitarian and philosopher rather than the son of God.

Reference: (http://www.bbc.co.uk/religion/religions/atheism/types/christianatheism.shtml)

616.

The human body contains energy equal to that of roughly 1.86 million kilotons of TNT.

Reference: (https://www.universetoday.com/114617/a-fun-way-of-understanding-emc2/)

617.

Keanu Reeves was forced to star in the critically-derided film The Watcher due to the fact a friend forged his signature on the contract agreement.

Reference: (https://www.theguardian.com/film/2001/sep/11/news)

618.

A massive typhoon would have seriously hampered the planned Allied invasion of Japan if the Japanese hadn't surrendered.

Reference: (https://www.washingtonpost.com/news/capital-weather-gang/wp/2015/07/16/how-typhoons-at-the-end-of-world-war-ii-swamped-u-s-ships-and-nearly-saved-japan-from-defeat/)

619.

Idaho has only one area code.

Reference: (https://en.wikipedia.org/wiki/Area_code_208)

620.

Kenyan author Ngugi wa Thiong'o' wrote his novel "Devil on the Cross" in secret, on toilet paper, while in prison.

Reference: (https://www.penguin.co.uk/books/1108477/wrestling-with-the-devil/)

621.

Jóhann Jóhannsson had spent a year writing the score for Darren Aronofsky's "Mother" and at some point realized that the film was better with no music at all. He convinced Darren to delete everything.

Reference: (https://en.wikipedia.org/wiki/Mother!#Music)

622.

According to the Peter Principle, anything that works will be used in progressively more challenging applications until it fails. Applied to a workplace, this means that "every employee tends to rise to their level of incompetence".

Reference: (http://en.wikipedia.org/wiki/Peter_Principle)

623.

Monsanto once created a town in Illinois so it could build a factory in a town with low taxes and lax regulations. The town is now home to a huge superfund site.

Reference: (http://en.wikipedia.org/w/index.php?title=Sauget%2C_Illinois)

624.

The "Bitch Wars" were between former Russian prisoners returning from World War II and the rest of the Russian prison mob who branded them as traitors.

Reference: (https://en.wikipedia.org/wiki/Bitch_Wars)

625.

Ryan Gosling was a child actor in 1996 Goosebumps episode "Say Cheese and Die".

Reference: (https://youtu.be/yr4qOIomCy4)

626.

In 1960, Miami was 90% non-Hispanic white, but by 1990, this figure was reduced to around 10%. This was mainly due to Castro's Mariel Boatlift of 1980, which brought 150,000 Cubans to Miami. This is the largest transport in civilian history.

Reference: (https://en.wikipedia.org/wiki/History_of_Miami#1980s_and_1990s)

627.

The video game, Mario Party 8, was temporarily recalled in the United Kingdom for using the word, "spastic," which is considered offensive in the U.K.

Reference: (https://en.wikipedia.org/wiki/Mario_Party_8)

628.

The movie "She's All That" was ghostwritten by M. Night Shyamalan.

Reference: (https://en.wikipedia.org/wiki/She%27s_All_That#Writing)

629.

The largest civil airship crash in history was not the Hindenburg but was actually the British R101 in 1930.

Reference: (https://www.wikipedia.org/wiki/R101?wprov=sfla1)

630.

When you pass out, your brain is unable to create new memories.

Reference: (http://www.youexplained.com/alcohol-affect-body-infographic/)

631.

Albert Einstein's adoptive granddaughter claimed to be his illegitimate daughter, a fact she couldn't prove as his only remaining DNA was untestable due to the embalming process used.

Reference: (https://en.wikipedia.org/wiki/Albert_Einstein%27s_brain)

632.

Ernest Hemingway survived two plane crashes in two consecutive days.

Reference: (http://www.monitor.co.ug/Magazines/PeoplePower/American-writer-survives-two-plane-crashes-in-Masindi/689844-3441866-q486coz/index.html)

633.

There is a furniture store IMAX theater hybrid in Boston, Massachusetts. You can shop for furniture at the entrance before the movie starts.

Reference: (https://laughingsquid.com/furniture-store-also-houses-an-imax-theater-trapeze-school-more/)

634.

Although St. Patrick is famous for ridding Ireland of snakes, there was no evidence of there being snakes in Ireland in the first place.

Reference: (http://www.reptilesmagazine.com/Snakes/Information-News/Did-St-Patrick-Really-Banish-Snakes-From-Ireland/)

635.

The "Can-Can" song was originally composed for an opera as a soundtrack to a man descending into hell.

Reference: (https://en.wikipedia.org/wiki/Orpheus_in_the_Underworld)

636.

Bart Simpson is a Canadian producer and filmmaker best known for the feature documentary, The Corporation, the highest-grossing domestic documentary in Canadian history.

Reference: (https://en.wikipedia.org/wiki/Bart_Simpson_(filmmaker))

637.

Having read a blog about his works published by a "Hip-Hop Literature Class" at High Tech High School in North Bergen, Kendrick Lamar came to the school to work with the students in dissecting his songs.

Reference: (https://www.npr.org/sections/ed/2015/06/13/413966099/a-visit-from-kendrick-lamar-best-day-of-school-ever)

638.

Twin brothers ran a marathon. Halfway through the race, they switched places in a toilet. The 1st brother drove ahead while his twin ran, rejoining the race ahead and finishing 9th. They were caught once a journalist noticed that the two wore their watches on opposite hands in different pictures.

Reference: (http://www.sahistory.org.za/dated-event/south-african-athlete-sergio-motsoeneng-admits-cheating-comrades-marathon)

639.

Hitler planned to rebuild Berlin after the war into a neo-Roman cosmopolitan city. One state building, the Volkshalle was to be so massive, that it could rain inside during events due to 150,000 peoples' perspiration and breath.

Reference: (https://en.wikipedia.org/wiki/Volkshalle)

640.

Cauliflower is part of the cabbage family.

Reference: (https://www.sciencedirect.com/science/article/pii/S0960982295000728)

641.

There's a special minimally-fermented wine used at masses where the priest is a current or recovering alcoholic.

Reference: (https://en.wikipedia.org/wiki/Sacramental_wine#Catholic_Church_norms)

642.

Mr. Hankey from South Park was inspired by Trey Parker's father, who told him that if he didn't flush the toilet, Mr. Hankey would come out and eat him.

Reference: (http://southpark.wikia.com/wiki/Mr._Hankey)

643.

Mr. Hankey from South Park was inspired by Trey Parker's father, who told him that if he didn't flush the toilet, Mr. Hankey would come out and eat him.

Reference: (http://southpark.wikia.com/wiki/Mr._Hankey)

644.

"Grizzly Man" Timothy Treadwell was a bear enthusiast and conservationist who for 13 summers lived among and filmed grizzlies, until being eaten by one with his camera capturing the audio of the attack.

Reference: (https://en.wikipedia.org/wiki/Timothy_Treadwell)

645.

The British successfully developed a flying Jeep during World War II. Also known as the Hafner Rotabuggy, it couldn't take off but was dropped from another aircraft and served as a way the British could drop vehicles for their infantry. The Jeep never saw action and was later canceled.

Reference: (https://jalopnik.com/the-brits-actually-built-this-crazy-flying-jeep-1585391382)

646.

The Northern Mariana Islands has U.S. Democratic and Republican presidential primaries, even though they don't vote in the general election.

Reference:(https://en.wikipedia.org/wiki/United_States_presidential_election_in_the_Northern_Mariana_Islands,_2016)

647.

Tony Tarantino is Quentin Tarantino's estranged father and a struggling actor. Quentin refuses to speak with him and says that his father is only trying to capitalize on his son's fame after abandoning him at the age of 2.

Reference: (https://en.wikipedia.org/wiki/Tony_Tarantino)

648.

Liquid nitrogen doesn't freeze your skin on contact.

Reference: (https://youtu.be/11XRspReAvI)

649.

There are two kinds of bacteria: pathogenic bacteria, which causes diseases, and spoilage bacteria, which alters the taste or smell of food. Pathogenic bacteria grow better at room temperature, while spoilage bacteria can develop even in refrigerated foods.

Reference: (https://www.fsis.usda.gov/wps/portal/fsis/topics/food-safety-education/get-answers/food-safety-fact-sheets/safe-food-handling/refrigeration-and-food-safety/ct_index)

650.

Cassius Clay was only TKO'd once in his amateur boxing career, by a man named Kent Green in the second round in 1958. Clay was 16 years old at the time and, eventually, it would prove to be one of only two stoppage losses in the entire career of Muhammad Ali.

Reference: (http://archives.chicagotribune.com/1979/12/16/page/276/article/the-shafting-of-alis-ghost/)

651.

There is a Patron Saint of the Internet.

Reference: (http://catholicism.org/patron-saint-for-the-internet-isidore-of-seville.html)

652.

Goats' horizontal and almost perfectly rectangular pupils give them a field of vision of 330°. This means that they can see virtually all but their own backs without turning their head. This gives them a much better chance of noticing a predator before it is too late.

Reference: (https://animalsake.com/animals-with-incredible-eyesight)

653.

A Philippine University houses more than 50 stray cats after a group of professors decide to care for them in response to instances of security bagging and killing strays that wander in.

Reference: (https://www.youtube.com/watch?v=Sp1cup7zqNc&feature=youtu.be)

654.

There is a Castle in the Czech Republic that has had a "Bear Moat" filled with actual bears for the past 300 years.

Reference: (http://www.castle.ckrumlov.cz/docs/cz/zamek_oinf_sthrza.xml)

655.

A puzzling suicide note of a man who jumped from the Golden Gate Bridge read: "Absolutely no reason except I have a toothache."

Reference: (http://themortempost.wordpress.com/2014/01/06/a-puzzling-suicide-note-that-has-baffled-psychologists-for-years/)

656.

On its way to Pearl Harbor, the USS Arizona rammed and sunk a commercial fishing boat, killing two crewmembers.

Reference: (http://www.historylink.org/File/5378)

657.

The World Trade Center's memorial pools are 31% smaller than the Twin Towers' actual footprints in Lower Manhattan.

Reference: (http://www.nytimes.com/2005/12/15/nyregion/memorial-pools-will-not-quite-fill-twin-footprints.html)

658.

Since 2004, Alex Rodriguez has bought every rookie who walks into the Yankee clubhouse 3 suits.

Reference: (http://ca.complex.com/sports/2015/06/alex-rodriguez-yankees-buys-three-suits-for-yankees-rookies-every-season)

659.

The Earth's shape is called an oblate spheroid.

Reference: (https://en.wikipedia.org/wiki/Figure_of_the_Earth)

660.

There was a political party in Canada whose platform included diverting federal funds to yogic flying research in order to procure world peace.

Reference: (https://en.wikipedia.org/wiki/Natural_Law_Party_of_Canada)

661.

The endangered pure whistling language called Silbo is native to the La Gomera Island in the Spanish Canary Islands.

Reference: (https://www.youtube.com/watch?v=C0CIRCjoICA)

662.

Some astronomers convert light data into audio data and actually listen to the light that the star produces.

Reference: (http://www.popularmechanics.com/space/a15478/fiorella-terenzi-acoustic-astronomy/)

663.

The Judas cradle was a medieval torture implement which consisted of a pyramid shaped seat which was slowly forced up the anus or vagina until the victim died of shock or infection.

Reference: (http://www.medievality.com/judas-craddle.html)

664.

On the day Buddy Holly died, Waylon Jennings told him that he hoped his plane would crash.

Reference: (https://www.youtube.com/watch?v=amUbKtIcXPo&feature=youtu.be&t=190)

665.

There's a flawless recreation of the original Star Trek sets in Port Henry, New York that is made and funded by an Elvis impersonator.

Reference: (https://en.wikipedia.org/wiki/James_Cawley)

666.

The made up word "ghoti," was pronounced the same way as "fish."

Reference: (https://www.englishclub.com/esl-articles/199909.htm)

667.

In 1970, members of Japan's Red Army Faction used samurai swords to hijack a Japan Airlines Jet and divert it to North Korea.

Reference: (http://www.theguardian.com/world/2002/sep/09/japan.jonathanwatts1)

668.

British Prime Minister Margaret Thatcher pleaded with Soviet President Mikhail Gorbachev not to let the Berlin Wall fall and confided that she wanted the Soviet leader to do what he could to stop it.

Reference: (https://en.wikipedia.org/wiki/Berlin_Wall)

669.

Steve Jobs used a tactic where he dropped an iPod into the water to see if there were any bubbles, if there were bubbles, he would ask his designer to make it smaller.

Reference: (http://uk.businessinsider.com/steve-jobs-threw-ipod-prototype-into-an-aquarium-to-prove-a-point-2014-11)

670.

Until late 1942, it was common for German U-Boats to provide torpedoed survivors with food, water and the direction of the nearest landmass. This ended when a U-Boat towing lifeboats and flying the Red Cross flag was attacked by a U.S. bomber.

Reference: (http://en.wikipedia.org/wiki/Laconia_incident)

671.

Wife selling was a traditional English practice for ending an unsatisfactory marriage. Instead of dealing with an expensive and dragged out divorce, a husband would take his wife to market and parade her with a halter around her neck, arm or waist, before publicly auctioning her to the highest bidder.

Reference: (http://en.wikipedia.org/wiki/Wife_selling_%28English_custom%29)

672.

The Flint Effect is a result of cities being so delinquent in solving murders they appear to be beset by serial killers.

Reference: (https://www.newyorker.com/magazine/2017/11/27/the-serial-killer-detector)

673.

The Flehmen response, or "stinky face", is when cats smell something they like; they open their mouths and curl up their lips because an organ on the roof of their mouths contains extra scent receptors that help them get a better whiff.

Reference: (https://www.youtube.com/watch?v=XBFP7NQ58v0&feature=youtu.be)

674.

Only 10% of the cells inside humans are human cells. The other 90% of cells, which are still necessary for us to live, are bacteria.

Reference: (https://www.youtube.com/watch?v=KXWurAmtf78#t=0m49s)

675.

Dungeons & Dragons (D&D) is banned in U.S. prisons.

Reference: (http://www.nytimes.com/2010/01/27/us/27dungeons.html)

676.

Leonard Cohen had a brief cameo in a 1986 episode of Miami Vice, playing Francois Zolan, a French-speaking member of Interpol.

Reference: (https://cohencentric.com/2015/06/29/leonard-cohen-miami-vice-guest-star/)

677.

The European Union alone accounts for 51.69% of all global aid; in 2016, the EU accounted for $178 billion of the total $344 billion spent on development aid, compared to $72 billion from the U.S., $40 billion from Japan, $15 billion from Australia, $12 billion from Korea, and $10 billion from Canada.

Reference: (http://stats.oecd.org/Index.aspx#)

678.

Each year after the last flight from the Amundsen-Scott South Pole Station has left for winter, the few remaining and isolated "winter-overs" will arrange a back to back viewing of The Thing from Another World, The Thing and the 2011 version of The Thing.

Reference:(https://en.wikipedia.org/wiki/Amundsen%E2%80%93Scott_South_Pole_Station#Operation)

679.

Due to not enough methane being in the atmosphere to counter the oxygen, the Earth went into one of its first ice ages.

Reference: (https://en.wikipedia.org/wiki/Huronian_glaciation)

680.

The United States accidentally destroyed Britain's first satellite after detonating a nuclear bomb in orbit.

Reference: (https://en.wikipedia.org/wiki/Starfish_Prime#Aftereffects)

681.

Angry investors in a Chinese zoo threw a live donkey and a sheep to the tigers because they were frustrated at not seeing a return on their investment.

Reference: (https://www.capitalfm.co.ke/news/2017/06/angry-zoo-investors-feed-live-donkey-tigers/)

682.

A Swede faced a world-record speeding fine of $1 million dollars after being caught going 170 KMH over the limit in Switzerland.

Reference: (http://www.bbc.com/news/world-europe-10960230)

683.

In 1957, the BBC created an April Fool's joke where they convinced the public that spaghetti grew on trees in Italy and Switzerland. To grow a spaghetti tree, the BBC reportedly told them, "to place a sprig of spaghetti in a tin of tomato sauce and hope for the best."

Reference: (https://en.wikipedia.org/wiki/Spaghetti-tree_hoax)

684.

The oldest tree in the world was killed by one man trying to figure out how old it was.

Reference: (https://www.smithsonianmag.com/smart-news/how-one-man-accidentally-killed-the-oldest-tree-ever-125764872/)

685.

Australian Don Ritchie talked at least 160 people out of committing suicide at Watson's Bay by offering them a cup of tea and someone to talk to. He was awarded a Medal of the Order of Australia for his efforts.

Reference: (https://www.pri.org/stories/2012-05-14/don-ritchie-australian-man-who-talked-over-160-people-out-suicide-dead-85)

686.

A young boy once pocketed a few giant African Land Snails while on vacation in Hawaii. When he returned home to Florida and got bored of them, his grandmother released them in the backyard, starting an invasion of foot long snails in Florida.

Reference: (http://www.wired.com/2014/01/absurd-creature-of-the-week-foot-giant-african-land-snail)

687.

Europeans traditionally swam the breaststroke, while Native Americans swam the front crawl. When two Native Americans won an 1844 swimming competition in England, newspapers criticized their barbaric, "un-European" form. Europeans refused to use the faster front crawl for decades.

Reference: (http://en.wikipedia.org/wiki/History_of_swimming)

688.

The Ford Family is still searching for the Punch Bowl Henry received for winning a 1901 race that helped launch his company. It was lost in 1951.

Reference: (https://wheels.blogs.nytimes.com/2011/12/15/edsel-ford-ii-wants-the-family-punch-bowl-back/)

689.

Instead of divorces, Inuit men would traditionally "swap" wives. Also, although having multiple wives was uncommon, multiple men would sometimes share a single wife between them.

Reference: (https://en.wikipedia.org/wiki/Inuit_women#Family_structure_and_marriage)

690.

In Japan, women give chocolates to men on Valentine's Day and the men reciprocate it a month later for White Day.

Reference: (https://en.wikipedia.org/wiki/White_Day)

691.

The "cheerleader effect", the theory that girls look more attractive in groups, is scientifically proven.

Reference: (http://www.socialstudent.co.uk/cheerleader-effect-proven-science/)

692.

Archduke Franz Ferdinand of Austria killed around 300,000 animals in his lifetime, including deer, bears, tigers, elephants and crocodiles, with specially made double-barreled Mannlicher rifles.

Reference: (https://www.pbs.org/newshour/world/8-things-didnt-know-franz-ferdinand)

693.

Alien Ant Farm crashed the third annual BET awards with the police shutting them down.

Reference: (https://www.youtube.com/watch?v=JNM2tV3PA_8&feature=youtu.be)

694.

Stephen Stills' 1970 self-titled debut album was the only album in rock history to feature both Eric Clapton and Jimi Hendrix.

Reference: (http://www.rollingstone.com/music/lists/100-greatest-guitarists-20111123/stephen-stills-20111122)

695.

In the United States, football coaches make more than the presidents of those colleges.

Reference: (http://sports.usatoday.com/ncaa/salaries/)

696.

A year before the Manson murders, Sharon Tate gave an interview in which she described a nightmare she had where a man entered her home, tied up her and Jay Sebring, and killed them.

Reference: (https://dangerousminds.net/comments/did_sharon_tate_dream)

697.

The first known instance of a railway was not in modern history. Written references place it as early as 600BC. The Diolkos, a grooved road paved with hard limestone, was used to roll ships across the land, saving long transport times on goods and assisting in naval campaigns.

Reference: (https://en.wikipedia.org/wiki/Diolkos)

698.

When Johnny Rotten's father demanded that his son cut his long hair, Johnny had it cut short, but dyed it bright green in an act of rebellion.

Reference: (https://en.wikipedia.org/wiki/John_Lydon)

699.

During the contested presidential nomination of 1924, H.L. Mencken journalist, satirist and misanthrope said, "Everything is uncertain in this convention but one thing: John W. Davis will never be nominated." He was nominated 3 votes later.

Reference: (http://www.politico.com/magazine/story/2016/03/1924-the-craziest-convention-in-us-history-213708)

700.

Florida has a law banning single women from skydiving on Sundays.

Reference: (https://www.kshb.com/news/local-news/water-cooler/no-unmarried-woman-can-parachute-on-sundays-is-just-one-of-floridas-most-bizarre-laws)

701.

Benjamin Franklin wanted to make the odor of farts smell good so that farting in public will become socially acceptable. Franklin wanted flatulence to be "as agreeable as perfumes".

Reference: (https://www.vox.com/2015/1/13/7533665/benjamin-frankling-farting)

702.

In many European countries they have "Social Supermarkets" that allow the poor to buy discarded goods from normal supermarkets at very cheap prices.

Reference: (http://www.npr.org/blogs/thesalt/2013/12/11/250185245/social-supermarkets-a-win-win-win-for-europes-poor)

703.

Mary Tyler Moore once offered a restaurant $1000 for a 65 year old lobster so she could return it to the wild. Rush Limbaugh then offered $2000 to eat the lobster. The restaurant denied both offers and kept the lobster as a mascot.

Reference: (http://articles.philly.com/1996-03-21/news/25638207_1_lobsters-spike-tracy-reiman)

704.

Outspoken draft activist critic and New York Times editor Henry Raymond, kept protesters at bay during the draft riots by setting up 3 Gatling guns at his office, contributing to protesters attacking the neighboring pro-abolitionist New York Tribune instead.

Reference: (http://www.nytimes.com/learning/general/onthisday/harp/0801.html)

705.

The Judas goat is a tagged goat used to find goat herds in remote areas. When the herd is found it is slaughtered or removed, and the Judas goat moves on to find another herd.

Reference: (https://en.wikipedia.org/wiki/Judas_goat)

706.

The Sudbury School has no grade levels or classes. Instead, students aged 4 to 18 are age-mixed and a system of certifications for using equipment are given out. These certifications require specialized knowledge and outlines of safety concerns. The certifications are typically restricted only by demonstrated ability.

Reference: (https://en.wikipedia.org/wiki/Sudbury_school)

707.

Six wastewater treatment facilities in South Florida have been discharging an average of about 360 million gallons per day of treated wastewater into the ocean for decades through outfall pipes located 1 to 3 miles offshore.

Reference: (http://globalsubdive.com/project/hollywood-sewage-outfall/)

708.

Charles Spurgeon, the famous Christian theologian, was against slavery and received death threats for it.

Reference: (https://www.thegospelcoalition.org/article/why-american-south-would-have-killed-charles-spurgeon/)

709.

A man, Denver Lee St. Clair, died after being subjected to an atomic wedgie by his 33 year old stepson.

Reference: (http://www.nydailynews.com/news/national/atomic-wedgie-kills-oklahoma-man-article-1.1570024)

710.

The United Arab Emirates has roughly the same road fatality rate per person as the United States, but more than 3 times the fatality rate per vehicle, meaning that the inhabitants of the UAE are just as likely to be killed as those of the U.S. but with one third of the vehicles on the road.

Reference:(http://www.who.int/violence_injury_prevention/road_safety_status/2015/GSRRS2015_data/en/)

711.

In 1977, we received a radio signal from space that lasted 72 seconds. To this day, we still don't know where it came from. It was called the "Wow! Signal!"

Reference: (https://en.wikipedia.org/wiki/Wow!_signal)

712.

France still controls part of "New France" in North America; the Islands of St Pierre and Miquelon off the Atlantic coast of Canada.

Reference: (https://en.wikipedia.org/wiki/Saint_Pierre_and_Miquelon)

713.

Elvira Taylor was a notorious "Allotment Annie" during World War II. She was discovered to have married six sailors at the same time. She was found out due to a fight between two of her husband's when they learned that they were both married to the same girl.

Reference: (http://www.heretical.com/costello/13gleftb.html)

714.

The Roman Empire didn't exist until after Julius Caesar was assassinated. His adopted son, Augustus, returned and overthrew those who killed Caesar, then Augustus established the Empire. Augustus lived to be 75 years old, passing the Empire on to his own adopted son, Tiberius.

Reference: (https://en.wikipedia.org/wiki/Augustus)

715.

Prostitution in Australia is legal in both the Western and Eastern regions but have differing legislation.

Reference: (https://en.wikipedia.org/wiki/Prostitution_in_Australia)

716.

There is a river Alph in Antarctica, so called because it runs under moraine and glacier, into the Ross Sea, as in Kubla Khan.

Reference: (https://en.wikipedia.org/wiki/Alph_River)

717.

Love addiction is an addiction to a relationship which is obviously unhealthy to one's physical, emotional and mental health but which one chooses to continue staying in because getting out of it seems too hard, if not impossible.

Reference: (http://talkitover.in/love/love-addiction-signs-to-look-out-for)

718.

In 1941, more than three million cars were manufactured in the United States. Only 139 more were made during the entire war. By the end of the war, more than half of all industrial production in the world would take place in the United States.

Reference: (http://www.pbs.org/thewar/at_home_war_production.htm)

719.

A killer whale at the Miami Seaquarium named Hugo, committed suicide by repeatedly bashing his head into the walls of his tank.

Reference: (http://theorcaproject.wordpress.com/killer-whale-orca-marine-parks/miami-seaquarium/)

720.

Superlambanana is a famous sculpture that is half lamb and half banana.

Reference: (https://en.wikipedia.org/wiki/Superlambanana)

721.

The marshmallow originally came from boiling the mallow plant found in marshes. It has little in common with today's sugary treat.

Reference: (http://www.huffingtonpost.ca/entry/marshmallow-comes-from-plants_us_598b0847e4b0449ed506e001)

722.

The year 1816 is known as the year without a summer.

Reference: (https://en.wikipedia.org/wiki/Year_Without_a_Summer)

723.

Frankincense smoke is psychoactive and incense may act as a weak drug during religious ceremonies.

Reference: (http://www.scientificamerican.com/article/mass-appeal/)

724.

Jean Lafitte, of Battle of New Orleans fame, wrote letters of marque to "authorize" all the ships sailing from his Galveston base as privateers. These gave the ships permission to attack any other ships. At its peak, Lafitte's base made more than $2 million per year, which is $32 million today.

Reference: (https://en.wikipedia.org/wiki/Jean_Lafitte#Galveston)

725.

As a child, Jack Black, whose real name is Thomas Jacob Black, appeared in a commercial for the 1982 Atari videogame "Pitfall!"

Reference: (https://www.youtube.com/watch?v=V0w5wyguqxE&feature=youtu.be)

726.

In 2017, Norway will be the first country in the world to shut down FM radio and go digital instead. Norway plans to switch to Digital Audio Broadcasting, since FM is eight time more expensive.

Reference: (http://thedockyards.com/20-facts-norway/)

727.

The term "junkie" comes from the fact that recreational heroin users in the early 1900s would collect and sell scrap metal to pay for their heroin.

Reference: (http://www.opioids.com/heroin/heroinhistory.html)

728.

The longest word in English has 189,819 letters and would take you three and a half hours to pronounce correctly.

Reference: (http://awesci.com/titin-protein-the-longest-word-in-english/)

729.

The leading cause of airplane accidents resulting in deaths is known as a CFIT, Controlled Flight Into Terrain. A CFIT is an accident where an airworthy aircraft, under pilot control, is unintentionally flown into the ground, a mountain, a body of water or an obstacle.

Reference: (https://en.wikipedia.org/wiki/Controlled_flight_into_terrain)

730.

Banksy was inspired by graffiti artist Robert Del Naja, who is known as "3D", who later become a founding member of the English musical group Massive Attack.

Reference: (https://en.wikipedia.org/wiki/Banksy)

731.

Certain plants emit alarm pheromones when grazed upon, resulting in tannin production in neighboring plants. These tannins make the plants less appetizing for the herbivore.

Reference: (https://en.wikipedia.org/wiki/Pheromone)

732.

Stu Rutherford, the IT guy who got roped into playing the character Stu in "What We Do in the Shadows," went on to invent special lightning technology that Taika Waititi used in the flashback scenes in "Thor: Ragnarok".

Reference: (https://www.stuff.co.nz/entertainment/film/98828190/the-kiwis-who-have-invented-a-way-of-stopping-time-in-film-at-least)

733.

There were 30 feet long sea cows called Steller's sea cows in the 1700s but humans drove them to extinction.

Reference: (https://en.wikipedia.org/wiki/Steller%27s_sea_cow)

734.

People in the U.K. believe that driving on the left dates back to the 1700s where travelers would keep passersby on their right in case they were a bandit. This meant that their sword hand was at the ready to draw if needed.

Reference: (http://www.2pass.co.uk/goodluck.htm#.VDB5lvldXh4)

735.

New Zealand's native Māori make up only 15% of the population, but over 50% of the imprisoned population.

Reference: (http://www.aljazeera.com/programmes/101east/2013/11/locked-up-warriors-201311481133704146.html)

736.

David Lynch was originally offered the chance to direct "Fast Times at Ridgemont High". He said it was a funny script but, "not really the kind of thing I do."

Reference: (http://www.vulture.com/2017/08/david-lynch-rejected-directing-fast-times-at-ridgemont-high.html)

737.

Giraffe patches can be seen via infrared as they act as "thermal windows" to aid releasing body heat and cooling the animal.

Reference: (https://giraffeconservation.org/faqs/)

738.

Some of the most dangerous hunting in the United States is the wild Hawaiian cow.

Reference: (http://modernfarmer.com/2014/09/dangerous-hunt-stalking-wild-rainforest-cattle-hawaii/)

739.

A man received 5 years in prison after being caught sprinkling his feces onto baked foods at a grocery store.

Reference: (http://www.dallasobserver.com/2006-01-05/news/the-poop/)

740.

Jewish Hungarian, Ignaz Trebitsch-Lincoln who converted to Christianity, became a member of British Parliament, became a spy for Imperial Germany, worked his way into the post-war German far right, met Hitler, became a Buddhist monk in China, and spread propaganda for Japan and the Nazis.

Reference: (https://en.wikipedia.org/wiki/Ignaz_Trebitsch-Lincoln)

741.

Boeing nearly ended production and sold the designs of the 737 due to financial difficulties and poor sales in the early 1970's. Only the scaling back the production of the 747 and the cancellation of the Boeing Supersonic Transport project allowed it to continue.

Reference: (https://en.wikipedia.org/wiki/Boeing_737#Initial_derivatives)

742.

The Archdiocese of Philadelphia suspended 21 priests in March, 2011, due to accusations of sex abuse or otherwise inappropriate behavior with minors.

Reference: (http://www.nytimes.com/2011/03/09/us/09priests.html?_r=0)

743.

Women won their right to vote when a Tennessee state senator's mother asked him to change his vote.

Reference: (http://www.alicepaul.org/who-was-alice-paul/)

744.

The Baltic Way is a 2 million person long human chain created in 1989 to peacefully protest communist rule in Latvia, Lithuania and Estonia.

Reference: (http://www.thebalticway.eu/en/history/)

745.

In 2013, a West African lab called Woelab created the world's first 3D printer made entirely of e-waste.

Reference: (https://motherboard.vice.com/en_us/article/mg7bwa/upcycling-e-waste-into-3d-printers-and-robots-at-togos-woelab)

746.

Albertville, France's electricity is powered by Beaufort cheese. Since whey is unnecessary to make Beaufort cheese, bacteria is added to the whey. This transforms the whey into biogas. This gas is then fed through an engine which heats water to 90 degrees Celsius or 194 degrees Fahrenheit to generate 2800 MWh per year of electricity.

Reference: (http://www.citylab.com/tech/2015/12/this-french-power-plant-runs-on-cheese/422034/)

747.

The galaxies in our galactic local group are being attracted by an invisible gravitational anomaly that is 10,000 times more massive than the Milky Way. It was dubbed the "Great Attractor."

Reference: (https://en.wikipedia.org/wiki/Great_Attractor)

748.

The majority of the prisoners of war who were forced to endure the Bataan Death March were Filipino.

Reference: (https://www.britannica.com/event/Bataan-Death-March)

749.

Hans Zimmer's "Spider Pig", from The Simpsons Movie soundtrack, entered the U.K. singles chart at #24. The running time for the song is a mere 1:04, making it the second shortest single to ever chart.

Reference: (https://en.wikipedia.org/wiki/2007_in_British_music_charts)

750.

During the Nazi occupation of France, Hitler did not destroy the Canadian Vimy Memorial and told the Allies that it remained intact. He did this because he admired the peaceful nature of the sculpture.

Reference: (http://en.wikipedia.org/wiki/Canadian_National_Vimy_Memorial)

751.

Serial killer and cannibal, Richard Chase, only broke into houses that were unlocked. If they were locked, he thought it meant he was unwelcome but if they were not, he saw it as an invitation to enter.

Reference: (http://en.wikipedia.org/w/index.php?title=Richard_Chase)

752.

There are 100,000 children in U.S. foster care waiting to be adopted. About 23,000 "age out" every year.

Reference: (https://www.bethany.org/adoption/foster-care-adoption)

753.

The first 1080 ever successfully landed on a skateboard was in 2012 by a 12 year old boy.

Reference: (https://en.wikipedia.org/wiki/1080_(skateboarding))

754.

It costs $2,350 to renounce a United States citizenship.

Reference: (http://money.cnn.com/2014/12/10/pf/taxes/expat-passport-citizenship-renounce/)

755.

A retired teacher who had been struggling for breath for months was amazed when doctors told him there was a pea plant growing in his lung.

Reference: (http://healthland.time.com/2010/08/13/how-can-a-pea-plant-grow-in-the-lung/)

756.

There is a Minecraft style statue of Soviet leader Vladimir Lenin in Krasnoyarsk, Russia.

Reference: (https://themoscowtimes.com/news/minecraft-lenin-statue-riles-russia-communists-59691)

757.

The blood flow to the brain during the thought process is so strong that it is enough for the head to outweigh the rest of the body if it was balanced horizontally before. This experiment was conducted by Angelo Mosso in the 19th century, but only noticed with the rise of neurobiology.

Reference: (https://www.npr.org/2014/08/17/340906546/the-machine-that-tried-to-scan-the-brain-in-1882)

758.

There was a kingdom in India which had a "Breast Tax" on women.

Reference: (https://en.wikipedia.org/wiki/Nangeli)

759.

The gang who orchestrated the greatest cash robbery in United States history, almost got away with it. They were caught when one of the thieves gave a friend a stack of cash with the original cash straps.

Reference: (http://robbermagazine.com/the-dunbar-armored-robbery-2/)

760.

Salps, a marine invertebrate, reproduce by "obligatory alternation." One generation reproduces asexually; the offspring then reproduce sexually.

Reference: (https://en.wikipedia.org/wiki/Salp)

761.

India's Mars Orbiter mission had a budget of $73 million, which is less than the budget of big Hollywood movies about space.

Reference: (http://www.bbc.com/news/science-environment-29341850)

762.

The concept of toed shoes was featured on Married with Children, 8 years before minimalist shoes were invented.

Reference: (http://marriedwithchildren.wikia.com/wiki/Episode:God's_Shoes)

763.

Ants enslaved by other ant species rebel against their masters by neglecting the work that they're assigned to do, and even killing the master species' young. The slaves may not be able to save themselves, but by rebelling they can protect nearby relatives from the same fate.

Reference: (http://discovermagazine.com/2013/may/05-how-ant-slaves-overthrow-their-masters)

764.

A cargo plane delay prevented the 2016 Northern Alberta Lobster Festival from being able to serve any lobster. Guests were given hot dogs to eat instead.

Reference: (http://www.cbc.ca/news/canada/edmonton/a-fishy-snafu-alberta-lobster-fest-left-lobster-less-by-air-canada-delay-1.3731350)

765.

Harry Potter is descended from a Wizard nicknamed "The Potterer" who made his fortune inventing potions that cured the common cold.

Reference: (http://harrypotter.wikia.com/wiki/Linfred_of_Stinchcombe)

766.

A chimpanzee named Frodo has impregnated his own mother, killed a human infant, attacked cartoonist Gary Larson, and beat the head of primatology, Jane Goodall, so badly that he almost broke her neck.

Reference: (http://en.wikipedia.org/wiki/Kasakela_Chimpanzee_Community#Frodo)

767.

The Parrotfish eats dead coral, and then excretes sand. This sand feces is also responsible for nearly all the white sand beaches in Hawaii.

Reference: (http://www.huffingtonpost.com/2014/03/29/hawaii-beaches-parrotfish-poop_n_5052935.html)

768.

A possible origin of the name Cerberus, the multi-headed dog of the Greek god Hades, is the Proto-Indo-European word ḱérberos, meaning "spotted". Hades' dog might have literally been named "Spot".

Reference: (https://en.wikipedia.org/wiki/Cerberus#Etymology)

769.

The "G-Spot" is actually the "Gräfenberg-Spot", due being named after Ernst Gräfenberg, who was the first man to discover it.

Reference: (http://www.independent.co.uk/news/science/mystery-of-the-g-spot-explored-785601.html)

770.

Faroe Island locals annually partake in what they call the "Grindadrap Grind" where around 1,000 Pilot Whales are slaughtered each year. The whales are chased into a harbor and killed by the locals with knives while their family members cheer them on.

Reference: (http://www.cruiselawnews.com/2015/07/articles/cruelty-murder-of-animals/cruise-industry-supports-mass-murder-of-whales-in-faroe-islands/)

771.

Nazi German authorities kidnapped and indoctrinated hundreds of thousands of European children who they considered to have Germanic appearance. Nazi authorities used their Germanic physical appearance to prove the Germanic roots of the children.

Reference: (https://en.wikipedia.org/wiki/Kidnapping_of_children_by_Nazi_Germany)

772.

Lululemon founder Chip Wilson named the company Lululemon because he was delighted in the idea that trying to pronounce the name, with its three syllables beginning with "l", would pose a special challenge for the Japanese, whom he enjoyed making fun of.

Reference: (https://www.huffingtonpost.com/stewart-j-lawrence/when-yogis-kill-the-grisl_b_1077457.html)

773.

FM-2030 is a man who had FM for his initials and believed that he would live to be 100 years old. FM also believed that by 2030, everyone will be ageless and have a chance to live forever.

Reference: (https://en.wikipedia.org/wiki/FM-2030)

774.

When Yvonne Brill, the inventor of the electrothermal hydrazine thruster for rocket propulsion, died, the first line of her New York Times obituary read, "She made a mean beef stroganoff."

Reference: (http://www.newyorker.com/news/amy-davidson/yvonne-brill-and-the-beef-stroganoff-illusion)

775.

During the Cold War, a Soviet Navy officer named Vasili Arkhipov, prevented Nuclear War by being the only one of the three officers aboard the nuclear armed B-59 to deny the launch of nuclear torpedoes, as a unanimous decision of all three officers was needed to launch.

Reference: (https://en.wikipedia.org/wiki/Vasili_Arkhipov)

776.

A hummingbird's heart beats over 1,200 times a minute when in flight.

Reference: (http://www.pbs.org/wnet/nature/super-hummingbirds-amazing-facts-hummingbirds/14543/)

777.

There are almost two times more kangaroos in Australia than humans.

Reference: (http://www.independent.co.uk/news/world/australasia/kangaroos-australians-eat-more-population-50-million-meat-animal-a7941076.html)

778.

There is no Nobel Prize for Mathematics because Alfred Nobel didn't want one.

Reference: (http://www.nobelprize.org/faq/questions_in_category.php?id=2)

779.

In the 1970s, people in Cambodia were killed for being academics or for merely wearing eyeglasses.

Reference: (https://en.wikipedia.org/wiki/Anti-intellectualism)

780.

The dog that found the last survivor of the 9/11 attacks was cloned.

Reference: (http://en.sooam.com/dogcn/sub04_02.html)

781.

The Stanley Cup has gone on "tour" in Afghanistan, where it briefly came under rocket attack. It emerged undamaged and has since been to Afghanistan multiple times.

Reference: (https://en.wikipedia.org/wiki/Stanley_Cup#As_morale_booster)

782.

The "Miss Cleo free tarot reading" psychic hotline was generating $24 million a month for two years straight. The Miss Cleo herself only earned $1,750 for the three days it took to film the first infomercial.

Reference: (http://www.vice.com/read/we-spoke-to-ms-cleo-about-her-fake-patois-and-getting-ripped-off-by-her-old-bosses)

783.

Marijuana is technically illegal in Amsterdam, but the law enforcement simply turns a blind eye to the "coffee shops" that sell it.

Reference: (http://en.wikipedia.org/w/index.php?title=Drug_policy_of_the_Netherlands)

784.

During World War II, about 250,000 Filipinos were promised U.S. Citizenship and Veteran Benefits for aiding the U.S. in fighting Japan. The U.S. reneged its offer after the war and only about 4,000 got any benefits at all.

Reference: (https://www.nbcnews.com/news/asian-america/forgotten-battle-thousands-wwii-veterans-are-still-fighting-n520456)

785.

The problems facing astronauts in space travel will be growing food. Plants have a statolithic, or gravitometric response to tell them "roots go down, stalk goes up" in the presence of gravity. NASA is experimenting to genetically modify plants to grow without this genetic response.

Reference: (https://www.nasa.gov/mission_pages/station/research/news/plant_gravity-sensing)

786.

In October, 2014, General Motors complained that the Flint water supply was causing corrosion at a local engine plant. General Motors switched back to Detroit's Lake Huron supply, meanwhile residents complained about the smell and taste of their drinking water, which they were assured was safe.

Reference: (http://www.wnem.com/story/26785625/gm-says-no-to-flint-water)

787.

The first commercially successful typewriter was built by an arms manufacturer and it looked like a sewing machine.

Reference: (https://en.wikipedia.org/wiki/Sholes_and_Glidden_typewriter)

788.

When Elvis' wife, Priscilla, didn't like a song that he and his buddy wrote and composed, Elvis never tried to write a song again.

Reference: (https://en.wikipedia.org/wiki/You%27ll_Be_Gone)

789.

In the "chicken poop prison" in Thailand, the ceiling of the cells was a grate, and chickens were cared for above the cell. Their dung was allowed to drop freely onto the criminal within.

Reference: (https://www.bangkokpost.com/travel/sightseeing/5535/khuk-khi-kai)

790.

When President Ronald Reagan was an actor during the 1940s, he had his mother sign his name to a lot of his fan mail.

Reference: (https://en.wikipedia.org/wiki/Autograph#Forged_autographs)

791.

Mob boss, John Gotti, would offer coffee to the FBI agents assigned to tail him.

792.

Both Gianni Versace and Gary Glitter had filmed cameos for Spice World. Their respective scenes were deleted for the December premiere after Versace's murder and Glitter's arrest for child porn.

Reference:(http://lostmediaarchive.wikia.com/wiki/Spice_World_Unreleased_Cut_Scenes_(1997))

793.

American gymnast George Eyser competed during the 1904 Summer Games despite his wooden left leg, winning the gold medals in the vault, parallel bars and rope climbing.

Reference: (https://www.npr.org/templates/story/story.php?storyId=93632621)

794.

It took mathematicians 358 years to successfully solve Fermat's Last Theorem.

Reference: (https://en.wikipedia.org/wiki/Fermat%27s_Last_Theorem#Sophie_Germain)

795.

Toyota and Honda have very simplistic designs for most of their cars because people tend to associate modern designs with high running and maintenance costs.

Reference: (https://en.wikipedia.org/wiki/Espinazo_del_Diablo_Formation)

796.

The Swahilian word "ua" means both "flower" and "kill".

Reference: (https://en.bab.la/dictionary/swahili-english/ua)

797.

Medical students in 18th-century Scotland could pay their tuition fees in corpses.

Reference: (http://www.historickilmun.org/stories/a-grave-problem)

798.

Napoleon once removed the Mona Lisa from the Louvre so that he could hang it on his bedroom wall.

Reference: (http://www.history.com/news/six-things-you-may-not-know-about-the-louvre)

799.

Titanboa, the largest snake in the world, has been reincarnated as a functioning robot. The robotic snake is 15 meters long and took four years to complete.

Reference: (https://youtu.be/LYe2ZOywtC0)

800.

Juan Pujol Garcia was a Spanish chicken farmer who was a double agent for the British during World War II, received both an Iron Cross and an MBE.

Reference: (https://en.wikipedia.org/wiki/Juan_Pujol_Garc%C3%ADa)

801.

The human body produces water, and has over 20 liters stored in its cells.

Reference: (http://www.merckmanuals.com/home/hormonal-and-metabolic-disorders/water-balance/about-body-water)

802.

The world's largest book is 1460 pages long, is from Burma, and is made entirely out of stone tablets.

Reference: (https://en.wikipedia.org/wiki/World%27s_largest_book)

803.

Buddha and the Laughing Buddha are two different persons.

Reference: (https://blavatskytheosophy.com/misconceptions-about-buddhism/)

804.

There was a court battle between two fans over who caught Barry Bonds's record setting 756th baseball. One of the fans spent $473,530 in legal fees to claim ownership of the ball. He only received $225,000 when the ball was sold at auction.

Reference: (http://news.findlaw.com/court_tv/s/20030709/09jul2003151330.html)

805.

New Zealand's famous jade is made of asbestos. It's a microcrystalline interlocking fibrous matrix of tremolite and actinolite, which are both forms of asbestos.

Reference: (https://en.wikipedia.org/wiki/Jade)

806.

The difference between a sociopath and psychopath is that a sociopath has a conscience.

Reference: (http://www.webmd.com/mental-health/features/sociopath-psychopath-difference?page=2)

807.

Eric Singer, drummer for the band "Kiss," was a juror for the Grand Prix d'Horlogerie de Geneve, the Oscars of watchmaking.

Reference: (http://www.bloomberg.com/news/articles/2015-06-29/kiss-drummer-eric-singer-to-judge-luxury-watch-awards)

808.

The Mona Lisa has the highest insurance valuation in history at $100 million in 1962, which is $800 million today.

Reference: (https://en.wikipedia.org/wiki/Mona_Lisa)

809.

A Muslim King from Guinea was taken to America as a slave. He was freed by Henry Clay and met with President John Adams before he attempted to go home and died 10 months later in Liberia.

Reference: (https://en.wikipedia.org/wiki/Abdulrahman_Ibrahim_Ibn_Sori)

810.

There's a town in Southern South Carolina called North.

Reference: (https://en.wikipedia.org/wiki/North,_South_Carolina)

811.

Billionaire Daniel Keith Ludwig had frozen his genetic material, believing that his estranged ex-wife's daughter might challenge his will. 40 years later, and after his death, she sued the estate and lost, because DNA analysis proved that he wasn't her father.

Reference: (https://en.wikipedia.org/wiki/Daniel_K._Ludwig)

812.

The world's oldest known dildo is a siltstone 20 centimeter phallus from the Upper Paleolithic period 30,000 years ago. It was found in the Hohle Fels Cave near Ulm, Germany.

Reference: (https://en.wikipedia.org/wiki/Dildo)

813.

Brazil has the largest Japanese community outside of Japan.

Reference: (https://en.wikipedia.org/wiki/Brazilians_in_Japan)

814.

The Thirty Years War was so devastating that an estimated 25% to 40% of Germany's population died from either famine, disease or battle. The male population of the German states was also reduced by almost half.

Reference: (https://en.wikipedia.org/wiki/European_wars_of_religion)

815.

The original of the song "As Time Goes By" from Casa Blanca has a first verse quoting "Fourth Dimension" and "Mr. Einstein's Theory."

Reference: (https://www.youtube.com/watch?v=Oo5mAg52ROM&feature=youtu.be&t=45s)

816.

In 2015, the U.S. exported $6.19 million worth of horse meat to Belgium, which was 85% of the U.S.'s total export of horse meat.

Reference:(http://atlas.cid.harvard.edu/explore/geo/?country=231&partner=undefined&product=660&productClass=HS&startYear=1995&target=Product&year=2015)

817.

The term "Fire in the Hole" originated with miners who wanted to let other miners know that they were about to detonate explosives.

Reference: (https://en.wikipedia.org/wiki/Fire_in_the_hole)

818.

Eric Cartman has been arrested six times so far in the show "South Park."

Reference: (http://southpark.wikia.com/wiki/Eric_Cartman)

819.

The commonly agreed upon number of aerial takedowns to become an ace pilot is 5, and the most recent American aviator to become an ace pilot did so in 1972.

Reference:(https://en.wikipedia.org/wiki/Flying_ace#Afghanistan_invasion.2C_Global_War_on_Terrorism_.282001.E2.80.93present.29)

820.

During Tool's concert at Garden Pavillion, owned by L. Ron Hubbard of the Church of Scientology, Maynard James Keenan spent most of the show baa-ing like a sheep at the audience.

Reference: (https://en.wikipedia.org/wiki/Tool_(band)#Undertow_(1993%E2%80%931995))

821.

In Turkish, turkeys are called Hindi, and in Hindi, turkeys are called Peru.

Reference: (https://www.youtube.com/watch?v=YDo6Jh67M0g&feature=youtu.be&t=187)

822.

Peanut butter is fluorescent.

Reference: (https://www.youtube.com/watch?v=fUnSpEtnDNw)

823.

The United States military has more aircraft than the next 7 countries combined.

Reference: (http://www.globalfirepower.com/aircraft-total.asp)

824.

Michael Bay received death threats for the Transformers movie because Optimus Prime's truck used flames in its paint.

Reference: (http://tfwiki.net/wiki/Optimus_Prime_(Movie)#Notes)

825.

The short-beaked echidna has a 4 headed penis.

Reference: (https://www.youtube.com/watch?v=vH3o2Q-YLPw)

826.

Humans can drink catnip like tea, and it has the same calming effect as chamomile.

Reference:(http://www.humanesociety.org/animals/cats/tips/catnip.html?referrer=https://www.reddit.com/r/aww/comments/4dhile/hugo_had_a_lot_of_catnip_and_sat_like_this_for_20/)

827.

Eminem was asked to star in the 2013 film "Elysium," but turned it down because the director wouldn't set the movie in Detroit.

Reference: (http://www.theguardian.com/music/2013/jul/18/eminem-di-antwoord-ninja-elysium)

828.

Before Joe Montana led a 92 yard game-winning drive in the Super Bowl, he was so calm in the huddle that he noticed John Candy in the stands.

Reference: (http://www.houstonchronicle.com/sports/superbowl/article/Greatest-Super-Bowl-moment-No-1-Hey-isn-t-10798680.php)

829.

A con man from Mali stole $242 million from a Dubai bank, by convincing the bank manager he could double money using black magic.

Reference: (http://www.miaminewtimes.com/news/closing-in-on-baba-6377878)

830.

Cows who eat food grown in soil with a higher contamination of heavy metals, have milk with higher levels of heavy metals, including lead.

Reference: (http://jcsp.org.pk/PublishedVersion/2724e2af-9fa1-469d-b922-03b2cf317687Manuscript%20no%206,%201st%20Gally%20proof%20of%2010624%20(Shahid%20Iqbal).pdf)

831.

Florence Nightingale, the quintessential English nurse, was born in Florence, Italy.

Reference: (https://en.wikipedia.org/wiki/Florence_Nightingale)

832.

When you become a citizen of Canada, you get a Cultural Access Pass that provides you with free admission to more than 1,400 of Canada's cultural attractions and discounts on travel.

Reference: (https://www.icc-icc.ca/site/program/cultural-access-pass/)

833.

A Japanese man responsible for beheading his master during seppuku failed to make a proper cut, which led to him committing his own seppuku but failing at that as well.

Reference: (https://en.wikipedia.org/wiki/Seppuku#In_modern_Japan)

834.

The infamous Josef Frtizl divorced his wife because she wouldn't visit him in prison.

Reference: (http://www.thejournal.ie/josef-fritzl-divorces-wife-649603-Oct2012/)

835.

Daria is a spin-off of Beavis and Butt-head.

Reference: (http://mentalfloss.com/article/73725/13-happy-facts-about-daria)

836.

Due to his baggage not turning up on time, Thomas Picton, the most senior officer to die at Waterloo, was killed leading a bayonet charge in his top hat and tails.

Reference: (https://en.wikipedia.org/wiki/Thomas_Picton#Death)

837.

The National Geographic Society was founded by Alexander Graham Bell's father-in-law. Bell succeeded him as President in 1897 and Bell's son-in-law in turn became the first full-time editor of the magazine in 1899.

Reference: (https://en.wikipedia.org/wiki/National_Geographic_Society#History)

838.

An investigation into the internal structure of Khufu's pyramid, the largest pyramid in Giza, has revealed the presence of a large and inaccessible "void" within the structure.

Reference: (https://gizmodo.com/stunned-scientists-detect-suspected-hidden-chamber-with-1820054009)

839.

In 1948, Hilton Tupman invented a horn that pedestrians could use to honk at motorists. He made it loud enough to be heard within a 1 mile radius.

Reference: (https://makezine.com/2006/11/08/pedestrian-horn/)

840.

Yitzhak Rabin resigned from being Prime Minister of Israel after a journalist discovered that he had an American bank account with $170 from when he was ambassador, which is in breach of Israeli law.

Reference: (https://en.wikipedia.org/wiki/Yitzhak_Rabin#Second_term_as_Prime_Minister)

841.

Dandelions aren't native to the America's.

Reference: (http://invasivore.org/2011/05/species-profile-common-dandelion-taraxacum-officinale/)

842.

There is a timeline of the far future, which draws on information from various scientific disciplines to predict events that will likely happen to our world, solar system, and universe through the next $10^{10^{10^{56}}}$ years.

Reference: (https://en.wikipedia.org/wiki/Timeline_of_the_far_future)

843.

All of the warring states near the beginning of the Old Testament were actually very small and only encompass what is now modern Israel.

Reference: (https://booksofthebible.com/p5388.html)

844.

In 1994, the world watched as fragments of a comet slammed into Jupiter, with one impact estimated to have released energy equivalent to 600 times the entire world's nuclear arsenal.

Reference: (http://www.astronomynow.com/news/n0907/16SL9/)

845.

There are ponds and lakes in Antarctica that, despite year round frozen temperatures, never freeze due to their salt content.

Reference: (https://en.wikipedia.org/wiki/Don_Juan_Pond)

846.

The term "suffragette" was first used by the Daily Mail, as a term of derision to describe activists in the movement for women's suffrage.

Reference: (https://en.wikipedia.org/wiki/Suffragette)

847.

Leonard Nimoy released multiple albums, including a two sided record titled "Two Sides of Leonard Nimoy". One side featured him singing songs as Spock; the other side featured songs related to his personal interests.

Reference: (https://www.stereogum.com/1784185/the-short-strange-music-career-of-leonard-nimoy/franchises/sounding-board/)

848.

In 1917, the U.S. Navy built a battleship in the heart of the New York City's Union Square.

Reference: (http://modernnotion.com/navy-built-battleship-heart-new-york-city/)

849.

Immediately after giving his famous "We shall fight on the beaches" speech, Winston Churchill allegedly muttered, "And we'll fight them with the butt ends of broken beer bottles because that's bloody well all we've got!"

Reference: (https://en.wikipedia.org/wiki/We_shall_fight_on_the_beaches#Reception)

850.

An episode of SpongeBob SquarePants in which SpongeBob was fired from the Krusty Krab caused a huge amount of controversy and backlash due to its depiction of unemployment.

Reference: (https://en.wikipedia.org/wiki/SpongeBob,_You%27re_Fired)

851.

The words for "work" or "job" in French, Portuguese, Spanish, Italian, and Galitian as well as the English word "travel comes from the Latin trepalium, which is a torture device using three stakes of wood.

Reference: (https://en.wikipedia.org/wiki/Tripalium)

852.

An Italian biologist named Francesco Redi performed an experiment wherein he removed the brain of a land tortoise, which then lived for six months. Furthermore, he cut the entire head off of one and it managed to live for 23 days.

Reference: (https://en.wikipedia.org/wiki/Tortoise#Lifespan)

853.

A city in France has the world's first short story vending machine.

Reference: (http://www.newyorker.com/books/page-turner/how-a-city-in-france-got-the-worlds-first-short-story-vending-machines)

854.

Video cassettes were still produced until 2015, the last company being Funai, which sold 750.000 VCRs that year. That's almost ten years after Blu-Ray was introduced, at a time when 230 companies were developing VR-related products.

Reference: (https://arstechnica.com/gadgets/2016/07/vcr-vhs-production-ends/)

855.

Andrew Myrick, a storekeeper on a Minnesota Native American reservation, told starving natives to get grass if they were hungry. He was found dead on the first day of the Dakota War of 1862 with grass stuffed in his mouth.

Reference: (https://en.wikipedia.org/wiki/Andrew_Myrick)

856.

In 1944, a 14 year old was executed by electric chair in the U.S. unconstitutionally.

Reference: (https://en.wikipedia.org/wiki/George_Stinney)

857.

shortest day of the rest of your life.

Reference: (http://www.radiolab.org/story/times-they-are-changin/)

858.

Duke Nukem Forever was mentioned in Wired's annual list of vaporware every year for 12 years straight. It was the number 1 vaporware title 6 times and was even given a Lifetime Vaporware Achievement award.

Reference: (https://www.wired.com/2011/06/duke-nukem-vaporware/)

859.

In the 1936 Olympic Games, boxer Thomas Hamilton-Brown lost his opening bout so he went on an eating binge to console himself. An error was soon discovered and it turned out he didn't lose, but was disqualified from competition because he had gained so much weight from binge eating.

Reference: (https://en.wikipedia.org/wiki/Thomas_Hamilton-Brown)

860.

The "Illegals Program" was a network of Russian sleeper agents under non-official cover whose investigation by the FBI culminated in the arrest of ten agents and a prisoner swap between Russia and the United States in 2010.

Reference: (https://en.wikipedia.org/wiki/Illegals_Program?BEF)

861.

The current Pope has a degree in chemistry and used to work as a chemist.

Reference: (http://ncronline.org/blogs/ncr-today/does-pope-francis-have-masters-degree-chemistry)

862.

The Sassanian King Khosrau I conquered Antioch and built a copy of it in his territory, where he transported its inhabitants. He called it, "better than Antioch, Khosrau built this."

Reference: (https://en.wikipedia.org/wiki/Ctesiphon#History)

863.

Many mushrooms and other fungi have four "sexes", or mating types, and some have even more than four due to multiple alleles.

Reference: (http://www.asmscience.org/content/book/10.1128/9781555815837.ch19)

864.

Most colleges and universities financial records are available to the public.

Reference: (https://www.citizenaudit.org/)

865.

In 1886, Major League Baseball pitcher Charles "Old Hoss" Radbourn became the first person to be photographed giving the middle finger.

Reference: (http://twentytwowords.com/first-known-photograph-of-someone-giving-the-finger-1886-3-pictures/)

866.

Jerry Lee Lewis tried to make a comeback after his scandal under a pseudonym, "The Hawk", in 1960. However, the radio station recognized his distinctive piano style and he was dropped.

Reference: (https://en.wikipedia.org/wiki/Jerry_Lee_Lewis#Family)

867.

Warren Buffett, worth $78 billion, gave his son Peter a single inheritance of $90,000 worth of stock at age 19. He has never given him more financial assistance. Peter spent the money on recording equipment. Had he kept the stock it would be worth over $70 million today.

Reference: (https://www.npr.org/templates/story/story.php?storyId=126538348)

868.

Black cats crossing your path is considered good luck in some places like England, Ireland and parts of Asia.

Reference: (http://fourleggedguru.com/black-cat-facts/)

869.

At the current oil extraction rate, we will run out of oil reserves by 2070.

Reference: (https://en.wikipedia.org/wiki/Oil_reserves#Estimated_reserves_by_country)

870.

There was a CIA plot to trick the Soviet Union into stealing bugged software, however, this led to the sabotage and explosion of a Siberian pipeline.

Reference: (http://www.telegraph.co.uk/news/worldnews/northamerica/usa/1455559/CIA-plot-led-to-huge-blast-in-Siberian-gas-pipeline.html)

871.

All Finnish taxi drivers must pay royalties for any music they play when a customer is in the taxi.

Reference: (http://www.complex.com/sports/2013/11/the-weirdest-driving-laws-in-foreign-countries/finland-taxi-drivers-pay-music-royalties)

872.

In February, 2011, Facebook censored the painting "L'Origine du monde" after it was posted by Copenhagen-based artist Frode Steinicke, to illustrate his comments about a television program.

Reference: (https://en.wikipedia.org/wiki/L%27Origine_du_monde#Influence)

873.

The preservation of the gene pool of the Ukrainian people is the duty of the State. This was mandated in response to the Chernobyl disaster.

Reference: (http://faolex.fao.org/cgi-bin/faolex.exe?rec_id=127467&database=faolex&search_type=link&table=result&lang=eng&format_name=@ERALL)

874.

Whales can't breathe involuntarily. If you anesthetize one, it will suffocate, even out of the water.

Reference: (http://nautil.us/issue/47/consciousness/the-kekul-problem)

875.

Before it was banned, a front flip long jump technique matched the standard long jump record.

Reference: (https://www.youtube.com/watch?v=RJ6ySgqjONI)

876.

In the 1910s and 1920s, a young man who dressed fashionably to attract women but didn't have much else going for him was called a "jellybean."

Reference: (https://en.wikipedia.org/wiki/Jelly_bean#Slang)

877.

American pediatrician, Saul Krugman, participated in deliberately infecting thousands of mentally disabled children with Hepatitis A and B between the 1950s and 1970s to further his research in vaccinology. He was later made the President of the American Pediatric Society in 1972.

Reference: (http://ahrp.org/1955-1970-saul-krugman-md-conducted-despicable-medical-experiments-at-willowbrook/)

878.

The longest TV show to ever exist is called Coronation Street. Created in 1960 and running to this day, Coronation Street has more than 9,300 episodes and more than 150 awards.

Reference: (https://en.wikipedia.org/wiki/Coronation_Street)

879.

George Washington, being the first president of the United States, did not get to live in the White House because it was still getting built.

Reference: (https://www.whitehousehistory.org/questions/who-was-the-only-president-not-to-live-in-the-white-house)

880.

The process that the meat industry uses is creating antibiotic-resistant bacteria.

Reference: (https://www.youtube.com/watch?v=ZwHapgrF99A)

881.

The U.S. Navy shot down a civilian airliner that was on route to Dubai from Tehran in 1988, killing 290 people, in Iranian airspace and waters.

Reference: (https://en.wikipedia.org/wiki/Iran_Air_Flight_655)

882.

In Ray Combs' final Family Feud, he told a player that got 0 points, "I've done this show for six years … this is the first time I had a person that actually got no points and I think it's a damn fine way to go out. Thought I was a loser until you walked up here, and made me feel like a man".

Reference: (https://en.wikipedia.org/wiki/Ray_Combs#Family_Feud)

883.

Pizza Hut, WingStreet, KFC and Taco Bell are all owned by a Louisville, Kentucky company called Yum! Brands.

Reference: (https://en.wikipedia.org/wiki/Yum!_Brands)

884.

Two kittens and three men crossed the Atlantic on a raft made of 9 telephone poles in 1956. The kittens were given to the Duke of Bedford, the Queen's cousin, and lived out their days in luxury.

Reference: (http://www.theglobeandmail.com/news/national/three-canadians-two-kittens-one-raft-a-little-known-journey-across-the-atlantic/article4462515/?herekitty)

885.

The first ever World Series of Poker Champion to qualify through an online poker site has "Moneymaker" as a legitimate family name. His ancestors were German coin minters who anglicized the name from "Nurmacher."

Reference: (https://en.wikipedia.org/wiki/Chris_Moneymaker)

886.

The last time the Olympics were in Korea, North Korean agents tried to derail the games by blowing a passenger plane and killing 115 people.

Reference:(https://en.wikipedia.org/wiki/Korean_Air_Flight_858?q=Korean+Air+Flight+858&_xt=EiQpmpmZmZkZLUAxuB6F61FYWEA5mpmZmZkZLUBBuB6F61FYWEA%3D)

887.

The De Rebus Bellicis, is a 4th to 5th century Roman pamphlet by an unknown inventor suggesting new weapons to save the Empire, including automatic weapons, paddle-wheel warships, armored transports for troops, and other things.

Reference: (https://en.wikipedia.org/wiki/De_rebus_bellicis)

888.

The Ontario Opportunities Fund is a fund where Ontario, Canada, residents can voluntarily pay more tax to help the government reduce their debt.

Reference: (http://www.fin.gov.on.ca/en/credit/oof/)

889.

There have actually been more than 400 earthquakes in Nepal since the first one struck exactly one year ago.

Reference: (http://earthquakes.possiblehealth.org/)

890.

Before he was a puppet, Yoda was going to be a monkey in a mask.

Reference: (https://www.theguardian.com/film/2013/nov/21/star-wars-yoda-monkey-lego-characters)

891.

The book Swastika Night depicted the Nazis winning World War II, two years before the war even started when Hitler invaded Poland.

Reference: (https://en.wikipedia.org/wiki/Swastika_Night)

892.

Pope Leo IV had a wall constructed around Vatican City.

Reference: (http://www.history.com/topics/vatican-city)

893.

Natalie Portman and Danica McKellar are among the 15 lowest Erdos-Bacon-Sabbath numbers on Earth.

Reference: (http://timeblimp.com/?page_id=195)

894.

"Steal This Book" is an instruction manual by Abbie Hoffman on, among other things, shoplifting, fare evasion, and protesting. 30 publishers refused to print it, and many book stores refused to sell it because people were shoplifting the book, as the title suggested.

Reference: (https://en.wikipedia.org/wiki/Steal_This_Book)

895.

Mont Saint-Michel is a massive castle town in the north of France that is only ever briefly connected to the mainland at low tide. Consequently, it remained unconquered by the English during the entirety of the Hundred Years War.

Reference: (http://en.normandie-tourisme.fr/discover/normandy-must-sees/the-10-top-normandy-must-sees/mont-saint-michel-106-2.html)

896.

For her role of Amy in Gone Girl, Rosamund Pike gained and lost 13 pounds 3 times to play the character at different times in her life. She consumed hamburgers and malts to gain the weight and exercised with a professional boxer for up to 4 hours a day and ran 5 miles to lose weight.

Reference: (http://variety.com/2014/film/features/rosamund-pike-gone-girl-2-1201316673/)

897.

A company in Japan offers a "baby bonus" of $400 for the first child and up to $40,000 for the fifth child.

Reference: (https://en.wikipedia.org/wiki/SoftBank#Baby_bonus)

898.

The online Oxford English Dictionary defines Eminem's song "Stan" as, "an overzealous or obsessive fan of a particular celebrity".

Reference: (https://www.billboard.com/articles/columns/hip-hop/7817376/eminem-stan-dictionary)

899.

Steve Jobs relieved stress by soaking his feet in Apple's company toilets.

Reference: (https://www.nbcnews.com/healthmain/strange-eating-habits-steve-jobs-119434)

900.

The U.S. Army was planning on training 2 million dogs to invade Japanese islands in World War I.

Reference: (https://en.wikipedia.org/wiki/Dogs_in_warfare#Fighting)

901.

When the Russian submarine, Kursk, sank in the Bering Sea with 118 sailors on board, Russia turned down offers from Britain and Norway to send a rescue mission, saying that the crew had been killed by an explosion. The bodies of 24 initial survivors were found in a compartment 9 days later.

Reference: (https://en.wikipedia.org/wiki/Russian_submarine_Kursk_(K-141)#Rescue_attempts)

902.

During the Papal election of 1292 and 1294, a hermit named Pietro de Morrone wrote a letter to the cardinals stating that they would be punished by God if there was any more delay. The cardinals, in turn, elected de Morrone as Pope Celestine V and sent for him. He initially refused and attempted to flee.

Reference: (https://en.wikipedia.org/wiki/Pope_Celestine_V#Election_as_pope)

903.

Adult children in China are required by law to visit their parents "often" and "occasionally" send them greetings.

Reference: (http://www.nytimes.com/2013/07/03/world/asia/filial-piety-once-a-virtue-in-china-is-now-the-law.html)

904.

There is a lightbulb that has been burning since 1901.

Reference: (http://www.centennialbulb.org/)

905.

For 12 days during the Battle of Berlin in World War II, a group of 770, 50 year old World War I veterans in the Bolkssturm militia held their district against the approaching Soviet army until they had just 26 rifles and 2 light machine guns left. 26 of them were awarded the Iron Cross.

Reference: (https://en.wikipedia.org/wiki/Volkssturm#Battle_for_Berlin)

906.

The Mexico City Subway has a symbol for each station.

Reference: (https://ggwash.org/view/62461/mexico-citys-metro-map-uses-a-different-icon-for-each-station-ours-almost-did-too)

907.

Silly String is used to detect tripwires in military operations.

Reference: (http://www.nydailynews.com/news/80-000-cans-silly-string-collected-troops-iraq-article-1.230724)

908.

In 1993, 24 British Nationals were killed in a raid on a Texas church by the U.S. Government.

Reference: (https://en.wikipedia.org/wiki/Waco_siege)

909.

Tracie Ruiz, the Olympian, won the 1984 Olympic gold medal for solo synchronized swimming.

Reference: (https://en.wikipedia.org/wiki/Tracie_Ruiz)

910.

Many elevators in Denmark have a button labeled "I fart", which translates as "in motion". When Queen Elizabeth II visited in 1960, strips of tape were used to cover these buttons in any elevators she used.

Reference: (https://www.teachers.net/gazette/MAR09/newlin/)

911.

Danny Greene was an Irish-American mobster who battled the Italian Mafia in Cleveland, and was ultimate assassinated via a car bomb in 1977.

Reference: (https://en.wikipedia.org/wiki/Danny_Greene)

912.

"Green around the gills" is used to describe someone who looks sick, especially someone who looks nauseated.

Reference: (http://grammarist.com/idiom/green-around-the-gills-and-green-about-the-gills/)

913.

While it's illegal to place weapons of mass destruction on any celestial body, it's perfectly legal to place "conventional weapons" in space.

Reference: (https://en.wikipedia.org/wiki/Outer_Space_Treaty)

914.

The original title of the first "Star Wars" film was "Adventures of Luke Starkiller, as taken from the Journal of the Whills, Saga I: The Star Wars"

Reference: (https://en.wikipedia.org/wiki/Star_Wars)

915.

Mackenzie King, Canada's longest serving Prime Minister, regularly conducted Séances to talk with his dead mother, former Prime Minister's, and his dead dogs.

Reference: (http://www.thecanadianencyclopedia.ca/en/article/william-lyon-mackenzie-king/)

916.

244 shows have come and gone on Fox since The Simpsons first debuted.

Reference: (http://www.screenjunkies.com/tv/tv-lists/244-fox-shows-that-have-come-and-gone-during-the-simpsons-500-episode-run/)

917.

The U.K.'s Oscars of Pornography are called the "SHAFTAS."

Reference: (https://en.wikipedia.org/wiki/Soft_and_Hard_Adult_Film_and_Television_Awards)

918.

The woman who voiced the female gargoyle in Disney's "Hunchback of Notre Dame" was also the live action reference model for Cruella De Vil in 1961's "101 Dalmatians".

Reference: (https://en.wikipedia.org/wiki/Mary_Wickes)

919.

The USS Akron was a U.S. flying aircraft carrier that caused the deaths of two Navy seamen when it starting floating upwards after landing, carrying with it four men who had not released their mooring lines and fell to their deaths.

Reference: (https://en.wikipedia.org/wiki/USS_Akron_(ZRS-4)#%22Coast-to-Coast%22_flight_and_second_accident_(May_1932))

920.

The jacket popularized by the first Prime Minister of India was featured in Vogue Magazine and became a fashion statement in the West. It was called the "Nehru jacket," and was popularized by the Beatles and worn by people like Johnny Carson and Sammy David Jr.

Reference: (https://en.wikipedia.org/wiki/Nehru_jacket)

921.

The fastest manned airplane ever built was the "North American" X-15, an experimental rocket-powered plane. One test pilot reached 4,519 miles per hour in 1967, a record which still stands. The X-15 could fly so high that 8 pilots technically qualified as astronauts, according to Air Force standards.

Reference: (https://en.wikipedia.org/wiki/North_American_X-15#Fastest_recorded_flights)

922.

Scientists observed a soundwave going faster than light, titling it mach-c.

Reference: (https://phys.org/news/2007-01-mach-scientists-faster.html)

923.

The Whopper Jr. was created by accident in 1963 by the manager of the first Burger King restaurant in Puerto Rico. The molds for the standard Whopper buns didn't arrive so he used a much smaller local bun. The result was such a success that Burger King adopted it worldwide and called it the Whopper Jr.

Reference: (https://en.wikipedia.org/wiki/Whopper#Product_description)

924.

The classic short story about the Harvard MBA student trying to help the Mexican fisherman originated in Germany.

Reference: (https://en.wikipedia.org/wiki/Anekdote_zur_Senkung_der_Arbeitsmoral)

925.

The United States Government forced the residents of Bikini Atoll to move to multiple uninhabitable islands to conduct nuclear testing, moved them back to a radioactive wasteland, and now has them living on a tiny island and off of subsidies.

Reference: (https://en.wikipedia.org/wiki/Bikini_Atoll)

926.

In 1944, Nazi Germany worked on a design for a fighter jet that would run on coal.

Reference: (https://en.wikipedia.org/wiki/Lippisch_P.13a#Design_and_development)

927.

Since World War II, all British tanks have been equipped with the means to make tea. This is because British soldiers used to have to get out of the tank to boil the water, wasting time and endangering the soldiers.

Reference: (https://en.wikipedia.org/wiki/Boiling_vessel)

928.

3-bromopyruvate selectively targets cancer cells, destroying their energy sources while leaving healthy cells alone.

Reference: (http://www.dayspringcancerclinic.com/3-bromopyruvate-and-dayspring-cancer-clinic/)

929.

In the 1950s, CBS had "Operation Rainbow" where they placed color televisions in stores and other public places to promote color televisions.

Reference: (http://history1900s.about.com/od/1950s/qt/Color-TV.htm)

930.

The "Anchoring Bias" is the tendency to use initially presented information to make subsequent decisions. It is a widely studied psychological phenomenon, useful in salary negotiation, haggling, and sales.

Reference: (https://en.wikipedia.org/wiki/Anchoring)

931.

Sperm cells can live for up to 30 hours after a man has died. The sperm can be gathered and used for posthumous fertilization.

Reference: (https://mosaicscience.com/story/post-mortem-sperm-donation/)

932.

Ada Lovelace was an English mathematician and writer. She's considered to be the first computer programmer as her notes on Charles Babbage's Analytical Engine describe an algorithm for the Analytical Engine to compute Bernoulli numbers.

Reference: (https://en.wikipedia.org/wiki/Ada_Lovelace#First_computer_program)

933.

There was an initiative to create LEGO Age of Empires II sets, but it didn't happen because there weren't enough supporters.

Reference: (https://ideas.lego.com/projects/52276)

934.

After winning a record $314 million in the lottery, Jack Whittaker had a series of unfortunate events, including his property being vandalized, his granddaughter dying of an overdose, a casino suing him for bounced checks and his house burning down completely.

Reference: (https://en.wikipedia.org/wiki/Jack_Whittaker_(lottery_winner))

935.

Harriet Tubman, in addition to organizing the Underground Railroad, served with the U.S. Army as a scout, spy, nurse and soldier during the Civil War, leading a raid with the African-American 2nd South Carolina regiment that freed over 700 slaves.

Reference: (http://www.libertyletters.com/resources/civil-war/harriet-tubman-civil-war-spy.php)

936.

Waterfall Glen Forest Preserve isn't named for the man-made waterfall located there. It was actually named after Seymour Waterfall, who is a former forest preserve president.

Reference: (http://dupageforest.com/Conservation/Forest_Preserves/Waterfall_Glen.aspx)

937.

You urinate more when you're cold because of an increase in your arterial blood pressure caused by blood being taken away from your extremities and crammed in your core. Your kidneys shed fluid to try and stabilize it.

Reference: (https://en.wikipedia.org/wiki/Diuresis#Cold-induced_diuresis)

938.

A 30-story hotel in Changsha, China was built in two weeks.

Reference: (http://articles.latimes.com/2012/mar/07/world/la-fg-china-instant-building-20120308)

939.

Eriq LaSalle and Wesley Snipes were in consideration for the part of Geordi La Forge on Star Trek: The Next Generation. Edward James Olmos and Yaphet Kotto were considered for Picard.

Reference: (http://memory-alpha.wikia.com/wiki/Performers_considered_for_Star_Trek_roles)

940.

There was a beauty pageant in the 1950s called "Miss Atomic Bomb."

Reference: (http://mentalfloss.com/article/52631/4-atomic-themed-1950s-beauty-queens)

941.

There was a beauty pageant in the 1950s called "Miss Atomic Bomb."

Reference: (http://mentalfloss.com/article/52631/4-atomic-themed-1950s-beauty-queens)

942.

A lawyer in Quebec requested a DNA test for a Tim Horton's "Roll up the Rim" cup to determine its "real winner" in 2006.

Reference: (http://www.cbc.ca/news/canada/lawyer-wants-dna-test-on-roll-up-the-rim-cup-1.621961)

943.

There is a hidden hare statuette in every episode of Inside No 9.

Reference: (http://www.digitalspy.com/tv/inside-no-9/feature/a821260/inside-no-9-series-3-reece-shearsmith-steve-pemberton-interview/)

944.

Japanese kana evolved from a shorthand for a "Gibberish Chinese Font" type writing system.

Reference: (https://en.wikipedia.org/wiki/Man%27y%C5%8Dgana)

945.

Vin Diesel has never met his father, and doesn't know what race he is.

Reference: (https://en.wikipedia.org/wiki/Vin_Diesel#Early_life)

946.

In 2006, Katie Melua gave a concert at 303 meters below sea level in one of the legs of the "Troll A" oil rig, earning a Guinness record for deepest underwater concert.

Reference: (https://en.wikipedia.org/wiki/Katie_Melua#World_record_holder)

947.

There is a species of blind cave beetle that is only found in five humid caves in Slovenia. Known as Anophthalmus hitleri, they are named in tribute to Adolf Hitler in 1933 when they were discovered. Their name has not changed since, as it is taxonomic tradition to not change the name of an organism after it is named.

Reference: (https://en.wikipedia.org/wiki/Anophthalmus_hitleri)

948.

A bowler was credited with a perfect 900 series on multiple occasions. The claims are widely disputed as the scores were rolled alone during a pre-bowling session.

Reference: (https://en.wikipedia.org/wiki/Robert_Mushtare)

949.

16 year old Ronda Rousey was a moderator of a Pokémon forum, and her username was mew182.

Reference: (http://www.sbnation.com/lookit/2014/9/3/6102133/ronda-rousey-pokemon-forum-moderator)

950.

Marcel Tyberg was a Viennese composer who, because of his 1/16th Jewish heritage, was killed at Auschwitz in 1944. Before his capture, he entrusted his scores to a close friend. The scores ended up in the U.S. but were untouched for decades. Within the last 10 years, his music was rediscovered.

Reference: (https://en.wikipedia.org/wiki/Marcel_Tyberg)

951.

Scientists encoded "Smoke on the Water" on a string of DNA.

Reference: (https://www.digitaltrends.com/cool-tech/dna-smoke-on-the-water/)

952.

Despite focusing on the story of its female lead, Disney's Frozen has more dialogue by male characters than females.

Reference: (http://polygraph.cool/films/index.html)

953.

Pakistani officials said that 10 people were convicted of shooting Malala Yousafzai. 8 were secretly acquitted and freed instead of serving 25 year jail terms. 2 are serving life sentences. There is a dispute about whether the 8 were ever really convicted or if more were arrested due to public pressure.

Reference: (http://www.npr.org/sections/thetwo-way/2015/06/05/412211887/pakistan-officials-most-arrested-in-malala-yousafzai-attack-secretly-acquitted)

954.

Bonsai is not a specific type of tree, but the Japanese art form of making trees look miniature.

Reference: (https://en.wikipedia.org/wiki/Bonsai)

955.

Eggs have markings in the European Union. The first digit from 0 to 3 shows the condition the hens were in from organic to caged.

Reference: (https://en.wikipedia.org/wiki/Egg_marking)

956.

In 1989, a major group of Conservative rabbis in Israel relaxed the Ashkenazi rules against eating beans and rice on Passover.

Reference: (http://www.cjvoices.org/article/the-kitniyot-dilemma/)

957.

Tickling can be considered abuse.

Reference: (http://www.handinhandparenting.org/article/tickling-kids-can-do-more-harm-than-good/)

958.

One of the greatest boxers of all time was called Sam Langford. He, like other greats, refused to fight because of his power. He fought until he was 43 years old, at which point he was almost completely blind.

Reference: (http://themalestrom.com/the-greatest-boxer-youve-never-heard-of-sam-langford/)

959.

When a man had a heart attack at a grocery store in rural Minnesota, 20 people lined up and performed CPR on him for over an hour and a half until paramedics arrived; he survived.

Reference: (http://abcnews.go.com/Health/96-minute-cpr-marathon-saves-minnesota-mans-life/story?id=13048099)

960.

MERS is a paper company owned by banks to dodge County and State fees in the Unites States. They dodge taxes in the billions of dollars per year.

Reference: (http://usawatchdog.com/trouble-for-mers-keeps-mounting/)

961.

The CEO of McDonalds is British.

Reference: (https://en.wikipedia.org/wiki/Steve_Easterbrook)

962.

Sony makes most of its profit from selling insurance. Although it's not sold in the U.S., 63% of total profits came from its insurance products in 2013.

Reference: (http://www.nytimes.com/2013/05/28/business/global/sonys-bread-and-butter-its-not-electronics.html?pagewanted=2&_r=1&partner=rss&emc=rss)

963.

Ariana Grande's anthem to female empowerment, "Dangerous Woman," was written by three men. The R&B or pop song was also originally pitched to Carrie Underwood as a country song.

Reference: (https://en.wikipedia.org/wiki/Dangerous_Woman_(song))

964.

An alternate color scheme being considered when the Golden Gate Bridge was built was a "bumble bee" striped design proposed by the U.S. Navy.

Reference: (http://goldengate.org/exhibits/exhibitarea1e.php)

965.

In 1935, Congress declared war on soil erosion and enlisted kudzu as a primary weapon. More than 70 million kudzu seedlings were grown in nurseries by the newly created Soil Conservation Service.

Reference: (http://www.smithsonianmag.com/science-nature/true-story-kudzu-vine-ate-south-180956325/?no-ist)

966.

Mount Everest is considered the "world's tallest trash heap" because climbers have created, 'glaciers and pyramids of human excrement befouling the high camps."

Reference: (http://science.time.com/2013/05/29/60-years-after-man-first-climbed-everest-the-mountain-is-a-mess/)

967.

All potatoes used to make fries from Five Guys are required to be grown north of the 42nd parallel.

Reference: (http://www.mashed.com/80154/untold-truth-five-guys/)

968.

The death of the son's character in Stephen King's Pet Sematary was inspired by the author's own real-life experience. He was able to save his son from a truck on a busy highway near their home but incorporated what could have happened into the book.

Reference: (http://villains.wikia.com/wiki/Gage_Creed)

969.

The Merck Manual, the bestselling medical textbook in the world, categorizes flatulence into four categories: the "sliders," the open sphincter, the staccato or drumbeat, and the "bark."

Reference: (http://www.merckmanuals.com/professional/gastrointestinal-disorders/symptoms-of-gi-disorders/gas-related-complaints)

970.

The perfume, Chanel N°5, has the highest budget for an advertising commercial ever produced, costing $33,000,000.

Reference: (https://en.wikipedia.org/wiki/Baz_Luhrmann)

971.

To become an astronaut in Japan you are tested in your ability to fold a thousand paper cranes.

Reference: (https://www.meanwhile-in-japan.com/how-japan-selects-astronauts/)

972.

Marie Stillman, regarded as one of the best female Pre-Raphaelite painters, was around 6 foot 3 inches tall.

Reference: (https://en.wikipedia.org/wiki/Marie_Spartali_Stillman)

973.

AT&T used to send bills to iPhone owners that listed every time data was transferred. This resulted in bills being delivered in boxes.

Reference: (https://en.wikipedia.org/wiki/300-page_iPhone_bill)

974.

R.L. Stine, author of Goosebumps and Fear Street, developed the characters and was also the Head Writer for Eureeka's Castle on Nickelodeon.

Reference: (https://tv.avclub.com/eureeka-s-castle-co-creator-r-l-stine-on-the-show-s-in-1798241856)

975.

Mexican artists Diego Rivera and his wife Frida Kahlo were communists. When asked to paint for the Rockefellers, Rivera created an ode to the USSR and Lenin. After refusing to remove Lenin, the fresco was promptly plastered over.

Reference: (https://www.diegorivera.org/man-at-the-crossroads.jsp)

976.

The Guri Dam alone supplies more than a third of Venezuela's electricity. However, due to a drought started in 2010, the water levels are too low to produce enough electricity to meet the demand, and the government has imposed rolling blackouts to keep the power on.

Reference: (https://en.wikipedia.org/wiki/Guri_Dam)

977.

When the recipe for clam dip first aired on television on the Kraft Music Hall show in the early 1950s, New York City sold out of canned clams within 24 hours.

Reference: (https://en.wikipedia.org/wiki/Clam_dip)

978.

Michael B. Jordan is named after his father, Michael A. Jordan. The "B" stands for Bakari, which translates to "a noble promise" in Swahili. Currently, he has no plan to name his future offspring Michael C. Jordan.

Reference: (https://www.youtube.com/watch?v=BOQ-wZQhZZo)

979.

At least 60% of miscarriages are caused by Chromosomal Abnormalities.

Reference: (http://www.parenting.com/article/seven-most-common-miscarriage-causes)

980.

During the 1982 Falklands War, Argentina planned to launch combat divers from Spanish soil to attack the British Navy stationed at the Gibraltar.

Reference: (https://en.wikipedia.org/wiki/Operation_Algeciras)

981.

The Tetris theme song is actually a 19th century Russian folk song called "Korobeiniki."

Reference: (https://en.wikipedia.org/wiki/Korobeiniki)

982.

The only medically proven cure for hiccups that does not require drugs or surgery is "Digital Rectal Massage".

Reference: (http://qi.com/infocloud/hiccups)

983.

Bird embryos start to develop dinosaur hands, but the fingers merge with the wing before the chicks hatch.

Reference: (https://www.youtube.com/watch?v=tmjd5b5g8oo&t=3m6s)

984.

The term "trickle-down economics" was coined by a 1930s humorist and highest-paid Hollywood actor, Will Rogers.

Reference: (https://en.wikipedia.org/wiki/Trickle-down_economics)

985.

One of the sons of Frank Herbert, author of Dune, was a gay rights activist who died of AIDS in 1993.

Reference: (https://www.qbd.com.au/brian-herbert/)

986.

Solidified pig blood is a delicacy in some parts of China.

Reference: (https://en.wikipedia.org/wiki/Pig_blood_curd)

987.

Yuri Gegarin, the first man in space, began life in a mud hut.

Reference: (http://www.bbc.com/news/science-environment-12875848)

988.

A British major went on the British version of "Who Wants to be a Millionaire?" and cheated his way to a million pounds sterling through the use of coughing from his wife and his friend, both of which were former contestants on the show, as a cheating method.

Reference: (https://www.youtube.com/watch?v=HeR4jS_IO7Y)

989.

Only 45% of the London Underground is actually underground.

Reference: (https://en.wikipedia.org/wiki/London_Underground?repost)

990.

James Doohan, Star Trek's Scotty, was shot 6 times during D-Day and had his middle finger amputated. He went on to conceal it on screen throughout his acting career.

Reference: (https://warhistoryonline.com/world-war-ii/james-montgomery-doohan-wwii-veteran-chief-mechanic-starship-enterprise.html)

991.

There are more than 500,000 pieces of debris floating or orbiting around Earth now. Most of them originated as parts of satellites and rockets.

Reference: (https://www.nasa.gov/mission_pages/station/news/orbital_debris.html)

992.

Walking through room boundaries, such as door, can cause forgetfulness.

Reference:(http://www.freakonomics.com/media/Radvansky%20Krawietz%20%26%20Tamplin%202011%20(QJEP)%20(1).pdf)

993.

The Sydney Opera House cost 1457% over budget.

Reference: (https://en.wikipedia.org/wiki/Sydney_Opera_House#Completion_and_cost)

994.

Despite being called "the pigskin," footballs are actually made of dyed cow hide leather. There is one company that supplies all of the leather for NFL balls.

Reference: (https://en.wikipedia.org/wiki/Football_(ball)#American_and_Canadian_football)

995.

The engine on the BMW M5 is so quiet that the company plays fake engine noises through the speakers to "remind" drivers of their car's performance.

Reference: (https://nytimes.com/2012/01/26/opinion/warning-the-next-sound-you-hear-will-not-be-your-engine.html?referer=)

996.

A man named Chris Voight, the executive director of the Washington State Potato Commission, lived off of 20 potatoes per day for 60 days straight.

Reference: (http://www.forksoverknives.com/getting-well-on-twenty-potatoes-a-day/)

997.

The only Academy Award that Star Trek: First Contact was nominated for was Best Makeup, but it lost to The Nutty Professor.

Reference: (https://en.wikipedia.org/wiki/69th_Academy_Awards#Awards)

998.

In 2006, 34% of young Britons did not believe Timbuktu, in Mali, existed and 66% considered it a "mythical place."

Reference: (https://en.wikipedia.org/wiki/Timbuktu#In_popular_culture)

999.

In 1985, Michael Jackson acquired the publishing rights to The Beatles catalogue. Much to Paul McCartney's dismay, Jackson owned the rights to over 250 Beatles songs. He sold half his ownership to Sony in 1995.

Reference: (https://www.billboard.com/amp/articles/columns/rock/7662519/beatles-catalog-paul-mccartney-brief-history-ownership)

1000.

All the gold ever mined in history would fit in a cube of about 20 meters on each side.

Reference: (http://www.bbc.com/news/magazine-21969100)

Printed in Great Britain
by Amazon